TEENS TALK ABOUT ALCOHOL AND ALCOHOLISM

TEENS TALK
ABOUT ALCOHOL
AND ALCOHOLISM

**Written By Students From
The Mount Anthony Union
Junior High School
In Bennington, Vermont**

Edited By
Paul Dolmetsch and
Gail Mauricette

A Dolphin Book

Doubleday

NEW YORK   LONDON   TORONTO   SYDNEY   AUCKLAND

A Dolphin Book
Published by Doubleday, a division of
Bantam Doubleday Dell Publishing Group, Inc.,
666 Fifth Avenue, New York, New York 10103

Dolphin, Doubleday and the portrayal of two
dolphins are trademarks of Doubleday, a division of
Bantam Doubleday Dell Publishing Group, Inc.

Library of Congress Cataloging-in-Publication Data

Teens talk about alcohol and alcoholism.

"A Dolphin book."
Summary: Explores the experiences of drinking alcohol
and growing up with an alcoholic, in the words of
eighteen young people.
1. Alcoholism—United States—Juvenile literature.
2. Alcoholics—United States—Family relationships—
Juvenile literature. 3. Youth—United States—
Alcohol use—Juvenile literature. 4. Alcohol—
Physiological effect—Juvenile literature. [1. Alcohol.
2. Alcoholism] I. Dolmetsch, Paul. II. Mauricette,
Gail. III. Mount Anthony Union Junior High School
(Bennington, Vt.)
HV5066.K53 1987 362.2'92'0973 86-16616
ISBN 0-385-23084-2

4 6 8 9 7 5

BG

We dedicate this book to all the kids
who live in alcoholic families

Authors

Susan Caffery
Jason Devens
Nate Koziol
Michael Mahar
Meg Miller
Josey Moon
Kim Peterson
Kristin Rancourt
Brenda Reynolds
Jason Roberts
Melini Rogers
Michelle Sandquist
Gwen Shorey
Shane Squiers
Tammy Squiers
Dan Turcotte
Heather Watson
Kim Whitman

Editors'
Acknowledgments

We want to thank the board, staff, and administration of the Mount Anthony Union Junior High School, in particular the principal, Ms. Martha Rudd, for continuous support and encouragement throughout the year in which it took to prepare this manuscript. Anyone who knows the difficulties of instituting anything out of the ordinary into a day in the life of a school knows our task would have been impossible to complete without their efforts. In this regard, we want to make certain to give credit for extra effort to secretaries Barbara Baroni and Lois Feenan, who knew where we were supposed to be more often than we did, and who managed to get us there when we weren't.

We also want to offer our appreciation to all of those people, both in and out of our community, who agreed to be interviewed for this work. Most of them are identified by name in the text, although some have chosen to be listed, or we have determined it expedient, to list them under pseudonyms to protect themselves or people they love. In either case, their contributions to our understanding and, we hope, to yours are incalculable.

We want to thank our agent, Helen Rees, our editors, Lindy Hess and Jim Fitzgerald, and our friend, Eric Rofes, for always being available for anxious calls.

And finally, we save our most warmly felt gratitude for the kids and parents who opened their lives and devoted themselves to this project. In our minds, their courage in the sharing of their thoughts and feelings for the betterment of others is unequaled.

PAUL DOLMETSCH

GAIL MAURICETTE

Contents

Introduction

Alcoholism in parents, left unchecked, can destroy the spirits of children. There is no "sometimes" or "maybe" about it. A notion often applied to children who live in difficult circumstances suggests that they can grow up and out of those circumstances unscathed. In the case of children from alcoholic families, it is not true.

Even those who live in families where the drinking has ended are not exempt from further pain. The hurts they received during the drinking stay in them as scars and tender spots that continue to hamper their happy growth and development and continue to infringe upon their friendships, school performance, and self-images —unless something is done to stop them from doing so.

Luckily for us all, the destruction of human spirit in children is seemingly never complete. We believe that the voices on these pages are testimony to that. Luckily for us as well, there is so much that can be done by adults and children alike to build that spirit.

It is time for us to act. There are so many children silently and permanently injured by parental alcoholism that we believe it is in all of our best interests to view those children as our own, not as "someone else's children" or "someone else's problem." If we can simply accept the idea that the quality of all of our lives is affected by their hurts, then we can act with the understanding that all of our lives will be improved by their relief. And if we do not do anything, we will allow the cycle to continue. We will watch them become alcoholics, marry alcoholics, or raise alcoholics.

What often goes unnoticed is that it takes so little to do so much. Really. All it takes is for adults to begin and to continue indefinitely talking about alcoholism in our schools, in our churches, and in our homes. All it takes is for us to approach kids with respect and sincerity, to give them opportunities to discuss, dramatize, and—maybe most importantly—to take part proudly in projects designed to help other kids who know the isolation, shame, confusion, and self-hate that are part and parcel of life for children in alcoholic families.

We are not suggesting that the solutions to the problems that arise from alcoholism and/or life with alcoholics are simple; we are saying that offering some hope is. Much of what poisons the lives of children grows from their shutting themselves off from the outside world. And much of what dilutes those poisons comes from the expression of the confusion and paranoia, the recognition that hundreds of thousands of other kids go through *exactly* the same feelings.

It has been said that alcoholics live in two different worlds. So do kids who grow up in alcoholic families. And just as no one can really ever understand what it is like to be in the alcoholic world without having gone through it, the child of an alcoholic world is best understood and acknowledged by those who have been there— and come back.

There is no greater pleasure than seeing the looks on faces of children who, for the first time in their lives, express the craziness they have held inside for so long and realize they are not alone, they are not to blame, there is another world out there. And it can happen in an instant.

There are so many kids who are ready for this experience. When we began this project there were people who suggested to us that we would have difficulty finding volunteers. They told us that parents and children would hesitate. We are sure there are some, maybe many, who did. Yet we received four times the number of volunteers we could involve—seventy-five—and this from only one grade of three hundred and fifty kids, from one school, in one small town. It was our greatest disappointment that there were only two of us and so many of them.

We have learned so much from the kids in this project. Not all of them have lived in families where alcoholism has been a problem. But all of them have seen the devastation that alcoholism can wreak on kids and adults—if not in their own families, then in families of friends and relatives. They took us inside the world of children who live in alcoholic families. And as a result we feel lasting bonds, not only with these kids, but with all who survive alcoholic families.

These kids, in particular, have done so much for others through the sharing of their thoughts and feelings. They have opened doors that will help others to know they are not alone. And we think that their offerings will demonstrate to all those adults who are in positions to engage kids in discussion and action just what they have to offer us all.

Writing this book was not easy or painless for any of us involved. But it was absolutely worth it.

This book is for both kids and parents. We hope that because of our efforts, there will be:

Fewer crimes
Less addiction
Less destroyed property
Lives saved
More agreement in families
More soda bought
More water drunk
Better decisions made by everyone

Chapter I

Who We Are

It is Friday afternoon, the thirteenth of December. John's week at school is over, the weekend finally here. For his friends it is time to party and enjoy themselves. Riding home on the bus, they all seem to be in great moods, laughing and yelling. John should be feeling that way, too, because he has been invited tonight to the birthday party of his best friend and, earlier in the week, his parents told him he could go.

However, John is not happy. He is, in fact, miserable. He is just sitting there looking out the window watching it snow and thinking about jumping off the roof of the school bus while it is rolling down the highway.

He is so miserable that when his best friend taps him on the shoulder and says, "If you look out that window much longer, you're going to have to put a quarter in it," John looks at him and tells him in Spanish what to do with himself. This makes his friend say, "All right, all right" and think, "Something must be the matter here."

What's the matter is that Friday is payday and payday means that John's father will be drunk and tell him he can't go to the party. John doesn't say that to his friend. He would like to, but he never has really told anybody about what Friday at his house is like.

As the bus pulls up to the stop, John and his friend get out and begin walking. All of a sudden John sees a van zigzagging up the hill. In an instant he turns to head in the opposite direction, but his friend grabs him and says, "Wait." John doesn't want to wait. He knows that in the van is his father, and John doesn't want to go home to what is waiting for him there.

John is thirteen years old, and his father is an alcoholic.

We Are a Group of Kids

We are a group of kids from the eighth grade in Bennington, Vermont, who are going to become authors; we believe we are lucky. What we will write about is living, in spite of alcoholism.

Writing this book is a big task, but it is worth it. Many of us have had parents, relatives, or friends who have suffered from alcohol problems. There are things that have happened to us that we would like to help others avoid happening to them.

We guess that we worry a lot; maybe too much. But we feel like we have to worry because we *know* that alcoholism is horrible and dangerous and *does* break up happy families.

Frank Jones, a thirteen-year-old boy we interviewed for this book, said, "Alcoholism can destroy a home. If you live with a drunken parent, you know what I mean. You really don't ever understand what is going on, and it scares you, sometimes so badly that you can't take it anymore and you leave. When there are people in the house who you still love, this is hard."

We think it is time to shut the door on the harmful effects of alcoholism on kids and adults; alcoholic teenagers and adults *can* get control of their drinking problems. Many have gotten help from doctors, counselors, and Alcoholics Anonymous and are recovering. And we want to take some responsibility in making that happen.

We Want to Help Kids Cope

Our biggest hope is that this book will help anyone who lives in an alcoholic family to cope with the mental and physical scars from lives in those families.

Alcoholism is a disease of denial, and people who suffer from this disease live in two different worlds: a sober world, where they are themselves and fun for kids to be with, and a drunk world, a world which is upsetting to kids.

You see, when you live in a family with alcoholics you think that you need to take the blame for crazy things that happen to you, things such as:

Physical abuse
Emotional abuse
Sexual abuse

These things make you feel ashamed and lonely, as if no one cares about you, and, at times, as if everything is your fault.

We want everyone who has these feelings to understand that there are others who care about them and know what they are going through. This is most important to us. As one of us said, "I lived with my stepfather, who is alcoholic, for nine years, and I would like to share my feelings about that in this book because I have become pretty knowledgeable about alcoholism. I just wish that I had a book like this available when I was going through my experiences of living with him."

Another reason we want to help kids cope is so that they can avoid having their lives wasted by their own abuse of alcohol. If you live in an alcoholic family, you do have a greater chance of becoming alcoholic than kids from families not affected by alcoholism. And there will be pressure in your life to drink:

Friends who will tell you, "Try it, you'll like it."
Parents who will teach you to drink too much.
Brothers and sisters who will set bad examples.
Problems that will feel too big to handle.

One thirteen-year-old boy we interviewed whose father is alcoholic said to us, "If you grow up in an alcoholic family and then see somebody with a drinking problem, you automatically wonder whether that will someday be you."

We believe it doesn't have to be, and we want you to believe that, too. In order to avoid it, though, kids need to do more than hope. We think they need to know the facts about alcohol and alcoholism.

Chapter II

What Is Alcohol?

Alcohol is many things to many people:

To little kids, it is a curiosity.

To teenagers, it is "cool."

To responsible drinkers, it is a relaxant.

To bartenders, it is a job, their lives.

To restaurant owners, it is a money maker.

To probation officers, it is a frustration.

To actively drinking alcoholics, it is heaven.

To wives and husbands of drinking alcoholics, it is a waste.

To recovering alcoholics, it is a painful old friend.

To us, it is something to be learned about and controlled.

Alcohol Is Not All Bad

Alcohol itself is not all bad.

In fact, it serves many useful purposes in things like cough medicine and vanilla, and in adding a tang to things you cook, like rum ice cream pie.

A lot of people who drink alcoholic beverages such as beer, wine, and whiskey drink them responsibly. Maybe they have one or two beers every now and then, or maybe they only drink a glass or two of wine on holidays such as Thanksgiving or New Year's. When they do drink, they have people who don't drink drive their cars home so that they don't kill people on the highway, or end up injured themselves.

Everyone who does drink alcohol doesn't become alcoholic. In fact, only one person out of ten becomes alcoholic.

Alcohol: Chemically and Socially

Chemically, alcohol is a colorless liquid that looks like water but has a mild odor. You can't drink pure alcohol, but different types of alcoholic beverages like:

Beer
Wine
Champagne
Gin
Brandy
Whiskey
Vodka
Rum
Scotch
Saki
Bourbon
And more

These have different amounts of pure alcohol in them. You can often tell that there are differences in the amount in each by its taste. Generally, though, this is the amount of pure alcohol that each of them contains:

Beer is 6% pure alcohol.
Wine is 12% pure alcohol.
Champagne is 15% pure alcohol.
Vodka,
Bourbon,

Brandy,

Whiskey, and

other hard liquors usually have around 50% pure alcohol.

Socially, alcohol is an acceptable and legal drug that can be purchased in beverages almost anywhere: bars, liquor stores, restaurants, and, in our state anyway, most any grocery store.

According to the law, not just anyone can buy alcoholic beverages. The law in every state in the United States says that if you are under a certain age you are not allowed to buy them. In most states you either have to be at least eighteen or twenty-one years of age.

Everyone can afford some kind of alcoholic beverage. Beer is usually the cheapest, followed by wine, and then hard liquors like whiskey. Some special beverages, like brandy, are very expensive. Kinds with classy names cost a lot more than regular brand names. Some imported wines can cost very much, too (the higher the quality, the more it costs), with some costing as much as thousands of dollars per bottle.

An average budget for alcohol in a household might be five to ten dollars a week, depending on the number of adults in the household. Usually it is not too much, if alcohol is not being abused.

When and Where People Drink Alcoholic Beverages

Beverages with alcohol in them are part of holidays like Christmas, New Year's, and Thanksgiving and special occasions like weddings, birthdays, and anniversaries. Or people will have some around for everyday kinds of events like a trip to a drive-in movie.

A lot of people are likely to drink a drink with alcohol in it in the evening when they are not working. If a parent works very late, on the night shift or something like that, and gets home when everyone is asleep, he or she might have a drink of something with alcohol in it before going to bed.

People typically drink more alcohol on Fridays and Saturdays than at other times of the week. They might have a beer or two when they are outside working and get very hot, or they might have wine and mixed drinks when they go to parties or out to dinner.

On Fridays and Saturdays a lot of people will go out to bars to be with friends and while they are there drink something with alcohol in it.

Bars are very popular places to drink alcohol. Kids usually have images of bars as stuffy places where drinks, soda, and juices are sold. They imagine that adults go to bars to get away from things for a while.

When we first thought of barrooms we pictured a lot of drinking and smoking going on and always the possibility of a fight. We imagined men trying to pick up ladies and some people drinking alone. We thought of crowded places that weren't the best places to be and we wondered why anybody would go to them.

Mr. Mike Mahar, the father of one of the authors of this book, has been in the bar business for twenty-five years, so we interviewed him to get an idea:

Us: Do you enjoy bartending?

Him: I did enjoy it, I don't do it so much now.

Us: What did your family think about your job?

Him: I think that when I was a bartender full-time it was somewhat of a strain. I worked late at night and I would be asleep when everyone else was up, and when I was up everyone else would be gone. It made it pretty difficult, actually.

Us: What do you think about alcohol in bars?

Him: Well, I think it is acceptable if it is used properly.

Us: What would you see as proper use of alcohol in bars or restaurants?

Him: I like to see people have a nice wine with their dinner. Late-night social drinking is a different thing. People drinking and driving is not good at all and should be something that is taboo.

Us: What kind of people come into bars?

Him: I think that everyone goes into a bar at one time or another.

I think that everyone goes out to drink socially at one time or another. They go out to have a good time, or after a show or whatever. I don't think there is anything wrong with that. I think the problem lies in places where the people have the wrong attitude about it. Some people drink so much that they refuse to admit that they are drunk and it can become a difficult situation.

Us: Do you think bars ever serve any social or community purposes?

Him: Absolutely. In a bar people get to know other people in a community; they get to talk over community problems. A very good community tavern, if it is used appropriately, is a good social gathering place. It is when alcohol abuse comes into play that you have problems in bars.

It seems like it can be a good idea to have a bar so that people can socialize while having a drink, if they drink responsibly. A bar can be a good place to listen to a band or to celebrate a birthday or an anniversary. It can be just a spot that you can have fun with friends.

Why People Drink

We asked some of our parents (who don't overuse them) why they drink alcoholic beverages.

Meg Miller said, "My parents tend to have a drink or two with alcohol in it during the evening. They drink it mostly because of its soothing, tingling taste."

Danny Turcotte said, "My mom said she likes a drink now and then because it does what she can't always do by herself—it relaxes her. She said that alcohol also releases her inhibitions, which means that she is able to let go of some of her uptightness with other people."

Michelle Sandquist said, "My parents only drink occasionally, but when they do it is for the 'goody sweet taste' or the atmosphere of being with friends while having a glass of wine."

Most people, it seems, drink to take away stress. Dr. William Pendlebury, a neurologist (a doctor who studies the brain) we interviewed, told us what alcohol does to make feelings of stress go away. He said, "In some people alcohol has a chemical effect in the area of the brain that controls feelings. This area is stimulated by the alcohol in those individuals and by doing that, people's feelings of well being are increased."

Stress is pain or suffering from pressure, and it can be both mental and physical. You probably know stress. Stress is the worry that comes when you are taking a test (or when you know that you are going to fail one!). Stress is having enemies who want to beat the living daylights out of you. Or, as Melini Rogers said, "When something really important is up to you and it really has got to be done right and you feel run down—that is stress."

Stress to your parents is a little different but probably feels the same as it does to you. Heather Watson, one of the authors of this book, came up with some examples. She said, "Let's say your father is the big cheese at his office. He has to worry about everything that happens there, and this means that when he comes home from work he usually is tired and frustrated. And when he comes home, you and your brothers and sisters are horsing around, your mother is tired from her day, and there is always something to fix.

"Let's say that your mother works, too, and on the same day she comes home from work to find your little brother staining (with grape juice) the carpet which she just cleaned the day before and the dog going all over the same rug."

The stress they feel makes their stomachs get very tight or their heads hurt or their muscles ache (or all of these combined). Before they face everything, maybe they have a beer or a glass of wine just to make those feelings go away, at least for a while.

We wondered, though, "While it is doing this, what is it doing to the body?"

Alcohol and the Body

This is the trip that alcohol will take if it goes through the body. First, it goes into the mouth in whatever beverage is being drunk. In the mouth, it will hit the taste buds and go immediately into the bloodstream (and to the brain). Then what is left after being absorbed there will go down the throat and into the stomach, small intestine, and liver, all the time sending alcohol to the brain through the blood. The liver will immediately start to filter it out, and as a result the alcohol will leave the body through the sweat glands or when whoever is drinking it goes to the bathroom.

Dr. Frederick Loy, a surgeon, told us that a shot of whiskey, a glass of wine, or a bottle of beer will all have the same effect and will all work at about the same speed on the body, but that the more concentrated the form of alcohol (whiskey is more concentrated than wine and wine is more concentrated than beer, for example), the more quickly it will be absorbed into the body.

He gave us an example of the speed that alcohol enters the system. "Alcohol that you put in your mouth will go throughout your whole body in less than five minutes. If you only put it in your mouth and didn't swallow it, it would still reach the bloodstream in measurable amounts in less than one minute. It acts very, very fast."

Alcohol, even though it makes a person feel good, is hard on the body. If the body could talk, this is what we would imagine the parts saying as the alcohol hit them:

Taste buds: "This is sour!"

Esophagus: "Get this out of here! What is it going to do?"

Stomach: "Reverse gears!"

Intestine: "Try to keep it in so we can get it out!"

Liver: "Oh, boy, here we go again. No more, please, no, not this. How long is it going to take to get rid of this?"

Brain: "Oooh, I am going to die young." (Slowing, going numb.)

Body: "Here comes a hangover!" (After going through the

sweat glands, and out of the breath. Body functions start to work again.) "Glad it is gone."

Alcohol will affect people in many ways, and all of their body parts will be affected by it:

Brain
Lungs
Liver
Kidneys
Heart
Nervous system

But the part that will be most affected by alcohol is the brain.

Alcohol and the Brain

The brain is the main organ in the body, the control center. It runs all of the body's organs and limbs through its different sections and it allows a person to think and make decisions.

Alcohol affects the brain by slowing it down. (We imagine that it makes the brain weak or hypnotized.) Dr. Pendlebury, the neurologist, told us that no one really knows the answer to why alcohol slows the brain, but that it does. He said, "Alcohol in general acts as a sedative. Sedatives have blocking effects on chemical mechanisms that allow the brain to function normally. It is probably alcohol's blocking of certain chemicals in the brain as well as blocking certain nerve endings that allows the alcohol to slow the function of the brain down."

Because alcohol slows the brain, it slows the control of the nerves, the muscles, and the senses. This includes the senses of:

Smell
Hearing
Taste

Vision

Touch

This can be a problem, because the senses tell people many important things. They tell people the difference between hot and cold and can help people sense danger. Even when you have just a little alcohol in your body you can't react as accurately to things that happen to you as when you have no alcohol. For example, as Tammy Squiers said, "When you drink, your senses might tell you that something is closer than it really is; or you might think a room is going around and around when it really isn't."

Dr. Loy said, "The Vermont state law says that if you have a blood alcohol level of .10 percent, which means that about one tenth of one percent of the blood in your body is alcohol, you are legally drunk.

"Now, I find that what I would call 'affected' results from levels quite a bit lower than that. We know that even one drink, an ounce of alcohol, will change a couple of things in your body, such as the ability to focus your eyes and the ability to adapt to light.

"For example, if you are in a dark room and somebody shines a light in your eyes when you have not drunk any alcohol at all, you will go blind for a couple of seconds. When you shut the light off, your eyes will adjust very quickly.

"But even a very low level of alcohol, less than the legal limit, will slow that down. That is one reason why even people who only have one or two drinks in an evening are a danger on the road in a car, especially at night. People will pass them on the road and shine headlights in their eyes. If they then drive along at fifty miles an hour blinded for only an extra second, they can go fifty yards in that second and possibly hit a tree, miss a turn, or run over someone."

When you are not sensing things accurately, the decisions you will make won't be very good. In order to make any decision you have to think over the things you have to choose from. If you have made similar decisions to the ones you are facing, you may think about what you decided then and this will make your choices a little easier. In any case, to make the decision you will have to think of the good points and the bad points of each choice and then choose the one you think makes most sense.

The problem is that just like a little bit of alcohol will affect your senses, a little bit of alcohol will cause your thinking to become foggy and may cause you to forget something important to making the decision you are trying to make. Dr. Pendlebury said, "If you have small amounts of alcohol, I would say the effect it has on decision making is that it slows it down. For example, if you had drunk a little alcohol, it might take you twice as long to figure out how to put a key in a lock as it would normally take you. But the more alcohol that you have in your system, the more likely you are to forget even how to put the key in the lock at all."

Alcohol and the Emotions

Alcohol affects the brain and it affects the emotions, too. Emotions are feelings. They are:

Happiness
Sadness
Anger
Frustration
Hatred
Excitement
Nervousness
Fear
Joy
Love
Delight
Hope
Despair
Disgust
Worry
And others

Alcohol will cause people's feelings not to work quite right.

Sometimes the alcohol will make people very happy and sometimes it will make them very sad (sometimes the way it changes people will depend on what they were feeling before they drank it). When the alcohol changes your emotions it can cause you to have abnormal responses to everyday goings-on. Maybe you will laugh at things that are usually not funny to you or you will say things you wouldn't normally say or maybe you will do things you have never done before.

According to Dr. Loy, alcohol has the same body effects on everybody, but different people may react differently to the same amount of alcohol. So just how much decision making and emotions will be affected will vary. He said to us, "If you and I each had a can of beer, it would effect you a lot more strongly than it would me. Hopefully, I could take in more beer than you without it bothering me because I am a little bit more used to it than you are. It is possible to get used to some of the effects of alcohol. For example, when you first start drinking alcohol it will make you sleepy, but if you drink often enough, some of the sleepiness effect will pass.

"Another thing that will make a difference in how you react is your body size. You are all pint sizes and I am a quart size. If you try pouring the same amount of alcohol into a quart-size person as you do into a pint-size person, it will have a different concentration, so it will effect the pint-size person quite a bit more."

**For Adults, Moderate Amounts of Alcohol
Will Wear Off and Won't Hurt
Their Bodies or Their Minds**

Alcohol has no positive effect on the body, but moderate amounts (one or two ounces per day of pure alcohol, which means one or two beers, one glass of wine, or one or two ounces of whiskey) are not going to damage adults' bodies permanently, and any damage that is done is completely reversible.

The effects of alcohol on their actions and emotions will wear off as their bodies get rid of alcohol by oxidizing it in their livers. To oxidize is to get rid of a substance by adding oxygen. The liver can oxidize about one half ounce of pure alcohol per half hour or about one ounce per hour. This is the same amount as a shot of whiskey, a martini, a mixed drink, one beer, or one eight-ounce glass of wine. If there is more alcohol in the blood after an hour, it circulates until the liver can dispose of it.

In fact, for some adults drinking a little alcohol each day may be good for them. Dr. Frederick Loy said, "I think that there is a real benefit to it. We know that people who have high-pressure jobs, like executives, do better if they relax during certain parts of the day because living under high pressure all the time shortens their lives.

"We know that a little bit of alcohol used every day will cut down on their strokes and heart attacks and by doing that, lengthens their lives. This is pretty well established. It is a good use of alcohol in moderation. Moderation means one or two ounces a day, at the most."

Alcohol is a drug that can be okay if adults know why they are drinking it and won't hurt their body's insides as long as they don't drink too much of it. As Dr. Pendlebury told us, though, "Any positive effects of alcohol have to be weighed against the potential for anyone to lose contact with what is a moderate amount of alcohol and go on to become an excessive drinker. I think it is easier today in our society when we live with the incredible amount of stress individuals have to deal with as they go through life. The time when all you had to worry about was whether the wheel was going to fall off the covered wagon is long since gone."

Too Many People Drink for the Wrong Reasons

When alcohol is not abused by adults, it does not become a problem. Sometimes a little alcohol can help parents stay calm if they had a hard day at work or a difficult day at home with the kids. In fact it can slow them down and keep them from taking out their frustrations on you. When this happens, families may have better times together.

But too many adults drink alcohol for the wrong reasons.

A lot of them drink to help themselves fit in with a group they want to belong to. Some even think that if they don't drink with a group they will actually lose their friends. Even adults are affected by peer pressure like this.

Mr. Gary Briggs, a police officer in our town, talked to us about adults and peer pressure. He said, "Adults have to deal with peer pressure. I have said recently that I don't intend to drink any more at all, even a glass of beer with a friend, because I really don't get anything out of it. I used to do it to be sociable when I was out with a friend or with another couple. Everybody would order drinks and I would go and order, too. Then, the next day, I would always wake up with a headache or feeling a little bit lousy. I just don't see any sense in doing that anymore."

Some adults drink to relieve themselves of serious family problems, to hide feelings that go along with them. They drink because they are lonely and depressed. Maybe they have lost their job, have nothing else to do, and may feel hate for themselves.

In fact, extreme pressure for long periods of time can often lead adults to abusive drinking. Connie Spencer, a thirteen-year-old girl we interviewed, gave us an example. "My father, after his mother and father died, has been blaming it on himself. Also, two years ago his first son and wife died in a car accident and he has been blaming that on himself, too. It seems that everything that happens that is sad he takes out on himself. For that reason, for the past year he has been drinking very heavily."

Often, when adults drink alcohol for these reasons, they get drunk.

Getting Drunk

Getting drunk makes anyone:

Dizzy
Delirious
Crazy
Hung over

Taking too much alcohol (more than body weight and experience will be able to handle) into the system at once means getting drunk, and getting drunk means having completely overdone it.

Dr. Pendlebury described what happens to the brain when someone gets drunk. "The brain works by communicating from one brain cell to another. It's like a computer. The computer is made of little chips that are wired together; the brain is made of little chips like connections that are wired together. The little chips of the brain are called brain cells, and the wires are chemicals that travel from one brain cell to the next.

"What happens when someone gets drunk is that the chemical messages are blocked, so that one nerve cell can't talk to another nerve cell. If you expand that to involve the tens of millions of nerve cells in the brain, it ceases to function properly."

Frank Stephenson, who is fourteen, said, "One Christmas night my father gave me a little bottle of beer and I drank it and got bombed out of my wits. It was strange, and I didn't know what was happening around me."

Being drunk is sort of like floating. It is like being in slow motion, in a dream world; everything is spinning and everything looks funny and hazy. People can tell when they are starting to get drunk when they start to see double and it is hard to move their muscles the way they want to.

Sometimes getting drunk will mean that they will simply act weirder than usual: sillier, tripping and stumbling like clowns; sadder, crying their heads off; or angrier, screaming at the top of their lungs. At other times it will mean that they will be acting totally stupid and foolish: swaying back and forth, walking in a zigzag way, and sometimes falling on their faces.

How they feel and act when they get drunk will sometimes depend on what kind of mood they are in before they start drinking. For example, if they are in good moods they will probably feel good. But, as Dr. Pendlebury said, "The quantity you drink makes a difference in how you will act, and how you are feeling at the time makes a difference. But there is a group of individuals for whom you can't predict what the alcohol is going to do. You could have someone who is feeling very happy, who goes to a party and for no apparent reason, even after drinking just one or two or three drinks (which would be considered a normal amount of alcohol), will become very, very depressed."

John Jones, who is thirteen, said, "My mother had a party once and I was making the drinks. Every time I made a drink for somebody, I would put vodka and orange juice in a glass for myself. I don't know how much I had to drink, but after a while I just started crying and I couldn't stop."

Whether people are happy or sad, once they start to get drunk it seems that they really just don't care anymore about what goes on around them. Jenny Colby said, "Once my mother and father threw a New Year's Eve party before my sister and I were born. One man there was allergic to martinis, really any alcohol. Well, anyway, he got really drunk and thought he could fly, so he got on top of the piano and tried to fly off. He fell and broke his leg and had to be rushed to the hospital.

"Another time that my parents had a New Year's party a man got really bombed and went totally crazy; he started doing all sorts of things, like getting fresh with the women. Finally, another man got fed up with his behavior and took him outside and gave him a bloody lip. He, too, had to be rushed off to the hospital. After that my parents never had another New Year's Eve party again."

What happens after people are drunk is that they get "hangovers." A hangover is really the process of the body getting rid of the liquor. It is recuperating from the damage done to it from the alcohol. A hangover is part physical and part emotional.

Mostly, a hangover is how people feel when they try to get up out of bed but can't because they can't stand any sort of noise. We interviewed a fifteen-year-old boy who was drunk the day before we spoke with him. He described his hangover to us. "It is a headache, major headache. I got up this morning about six and I was totally dehydrated. I am pretty dehydrated right now because I really didn't get anything to drink all day, and I had to spend the whole day in in-school suspension just so that I could catch up on my sleep."

We wondered why, if all these things happen to people when they get drunk, they would keep drinking. Dr. Loy said, "We really should have some instincts that we are taking in a poison when we drink alcohol. But I think that it sort of numbs you so that you drink it automatically, thinking that if you take another drink it will make you feel even better than the first one. I think you are so numb that you sort of just reach for the next one."

Chapter III

Drinking and You

Becoming a Teenager

Becoming a teenager means you are getting older. It means going through puberty, and that can be full of growing pains or it can be fun.

When you become a teenager you expect to have fun, all kinds of fun. You expect to do things like:

Stay up until one o'clock in the morning

Chase your friends around town

Go on trips with your class

Do things on your own, like going to the movies

Just how many of these you can do depends on what your parents are like (or what moods they are in!). Usually, though, you can do more of these things when you become a teenager than when you were younger.

But becoming a teenager can be very disappointing, for one thing because you very quickly get used to all the new things you can do (it actually seems more exciting to turn from nine to ten than it does to turn from twelve to thirteen). For another thing, when you become a teenager you start getting more responsibilities!

It seems as if the day you turn thirteen your parents all of a sudden start saying things to you like, "Well, you are old enough now, you can start doing the dusting" or the sweeping, or the dishes, or the floors, or the laundry. It can almost make you want to become twelve again.

The most disappointing thing about becoming a teenager is that you imagined being able to go *wherever* you wanted to, *whenever* you wanted to, and with *whoever* you wanted to. When you finally do become a teenager, you find out quickly that your parents are still going to hand out rules.

In fact, it almost seems as if they have become more overprotective than ever. Sometimes you find out that you can't even do things you used to be able to do when you were a kid. Things like:

Fight with your little brother (you might hurt him!)

Go over to your girlfriend's or boyfriend's house (you might you-know-what!)

Stay out as late as you used to (you might get arrested!)

It seems as if your parents are afraid that if you do all these things you will grow up to be a horribly bad person. Restrictions make sense as long as they are not overrestrictions, but once you become a teenager you sort of get sick of all of them—even if they *are* "good for you."

Being a Parent of a Teenager
Must Be Miserable

When we think about it, though, it is possible that being the parent of a teenager is harder than being a teenager (it may even be miserable), because parents always have to be worrying about you, and you are always giving them the worst time.

It just seems that part of becoming a teenager is having a hard time with your parents. They start to seem really weird to you. Let's say you have a new girlfriend (or boyfriend) who you're dying to tell somebody about. You might want to tell your parents (like you did when you were little), but now you're afraid they will tease you about it (which they usually do). So you just don't tell them anything, which makes them think you're keeping things from them (which you are).

Some of our parents seem like they are going to get ulcers just from being afraid of what might happen to us. This is strange, because *we* aren't really worrying about what we're doing at all. The only thing *we* worry about is what our parents are going to say when they find out some of the things we have done!

Maybe that's why parents get overprotective at times. Maybe they worry too much about us because they think that becoming a teenager in America today is hard and dangerous.

Which maybe it is. Because once you become a teenager it seems like you are always struggling with:

Not being one of the crowd
Fighting with friends
Problems at home
Problems at school

Once you become a teenager it seems like there are a lot of hard decisions to make, like whether to take drugs or drink alcohol. These *are* very hard decisions in kids' minds, and the pressures to make them are very real.

Your First Expectation Is to Try New Things

Like we said, one of the first expectations of becoming a teen-ager *is* to try new things.

The truth is that one of the first things you think about trying is drinking. Sometimes you sit at home in your room and think, "I wonder what it would be like to get drunk?"

Since as a kid in America you aren't permitted to drink, there is a dare to do it that makes you think there must be something wonderful about it.

Actually you get really confused about drinking, because while you aren't being allowed to drink by law you are getting encouraged to drink by:

Television
Movies
Friends

Television commercials are always trying to get you interested in alcohol: "Genesee—Come visit the great outdoors in a glass." Or "Michelob Light for the winners." They always make you think about clean mountain air or tough-looking cowboys. They make drinking look really neat. If you are young you especially love the cowboys.

Movies do it differently: In the movies, you see guys drinking who are handsome and popular, and girls drinking who are pretty. You see this and it makes you say to yourself, "Well, I am popular, so it must be okay for me to drink, too."

Encouragement to drink from friends is the worst. They can really put a lot of pressure on you. Maybe they call you chicken if you don't want to drink. Just to get you to drink they will give you a lot of stupid ideas about drinking, like:

If you take a drink, you will feel big and tough.

One drink won't hurt you.

It will make you feel older.

The thing is that if a friend of yours has experimented with alcohol, you might be likely to do the same whether you really want to or not.

How You Might Start to Drink

Kids might begin experimenting with alcohol at any age: twelve, thirteen, fourteen, fifteen, or whatever. We would guess, from what we have seen, that seven out of ten kids try drinking at some time or another while they are teenagers.

Some begin drinking at home when their parents decide that they are responsible. Maybe they get their first drinks on special occasions like weddings, Thanksgiving, Christmas, or New Year's.

Most kids, even though it is illegal, start drinking with friends when they all want to experiment. That may be what will happen to you, because this is a common way that kids first experiment with drinking.

How Kids Get Alcohol

Kids can't buy alcohol legally because they are too young, but some people who are allowed to buy it will give it or sell it to them. It is really very easy for teenagers to get alcohol on the streets, too easy.

Jim, a fifteen-year-old boy we interviewed, told us how easy it is. "You just go in stores and get it. I know a couple stores where anyone could get served. The owners don't care, just as long as they get their money.

"Another thing kids do is just sit on the street corner and ask an adult to get it for them. I have done that a couple of times. Maybe I have had to give him five bucks, but it is no problem.

"Or if that doesn't work kids can head for Main Street and bum a beer here and there. There will always be kids cruising around with it."

Kathy, another sixteen-year-old we interviewed, talked to us about other ways kids get alcohol, "I think most kids drink, usually on Friday or Saturday nights; at least that's the way it seems to me. They drink mostly beer. Someone will get a couple of kegs and bring them to the parties. Other kids at the parties will use their allowances or leftover lunch money to help buy them.

"I also know a lot of kids at school who have fake identification cards who can get served at restaurants, bars, or anything like that. That is how a lot of girls do it, anyway.

"If kids feel real desperate for it they will steal it, a lot of times from their parents. Let's say that their fathers drink beer—not so that they are alcoholic, but if they have a couple while they watch football games or something, they may have it in the refrigerator. A lot of times the kids will get to it before their parents do."

Pressure at Parties

The older you get (fifteen or sixteen), the more chances you will have to go to beer parties. The parties are where most of the pressure to drink will happen.

You will probably go to parties because they are fun and because you would feel as if you missed something if all of your friends were going to be at them and you weren't.

At a party there will be a *lot* of pressure on you to drink. Sometimes as we said before the pressure will come from friends who are pushing you. But sometimes the pressure will come from inside you because:

You want to be "cool."
You want to feel "big."
You want to make more friends.

What happens is that you will look around and see that everybody else has a drink and you don't, which will make you feel like a jerk.

This is when you might pick up a drink just to have a good time, and to feel like no one is now looking at you anymore. You see, every kid really wants to fit in with the crowd. Nobody likes to feel left out. When you feel this way it is very easy to drink. What happens though is that it is very easy to drink and drink and drink. The pressure at parties is just so great to drink and kids know so little about responsible drinking.

Getting Drunk

To kids, getting drunk means drinking all the alcohol they can get. To most kids it means going out and drinking until they can't think straight anymore, because, according to kids' thinking, to have a good time drinking is to get drunk. It is the best way to be "cool."

Some of us have gotten drunk before. The first time you do, you think, "Wow, I finally got drunk." This is a problem though because if you are a teenager you are at risk when you get drunk. Adults don't often know what they are doing when they are drunk, but teenagers know even less because their brains just aren't fully developed yet. It is much easier for you to get hooked on alcohol than it is for adults. And when your drinking starts to get out of control, it will get out of control much faster than an adult's.

To show what we mean, we interviewed Jim, a fifteen-year-old boy, who the day before we interviewed him, got drunk at a party and was arrested. This is what he told us:

"There is this kid in town who has a party every Monday, Wednesday, and Friday from one-thirty to four-thirty. Everybody has to be out of the house by four forty-five because that is when his mother comes home. From what I can remember about yesterday there were about thirty or forty kids who were at this party, and they were all drinking.

"I usually drink about five times a month, which really isn't that much compared to what other kids drink. I know a whole lot of kids who drink more than I do, like every day after school.

"There is probably more drinking in high school than there is in college, and most of the kids who do drink don't get caught. A lot of kids I know drink whenever, whatever, and as much as they can get their hands on. If they get six-packs of beer they will drink them. If they have fifths of whiskey, they will drink them.

"Most kids drink with friends, but some will stash the stuff in their coats or hoist it up in their windows. They might have a few drinks before they go to bed at night.

"Any family can produce kids who drink. I know a couple of kids who drink because their family lives aren't too hot, but I know a lot of kids who drink just to drink. Once they start drinking, they get to where they like it. It puts them on cloud nine for a while and helps them to get away from life: the pressure from school, home, and friends.

"Every kid knows where the parties are, whose parents aren't going to be home, and whose parents are on vacation. Every day people run around school saying, 'Where's the party? Where's the party?' By afternoon most everybody knows.

"What happened to me yesterday happened mainly because of peer pressure. I didn't want to drink, but somebody held a shot glass over me and said, 'Oh come on, are you chicken?' Then that was it. I just took the glass. I don't like dares, and when there are fifteen or twenty kids in a room calling me chicken, the only way I can get them to stop is to drink.

"This was my first encounter with hard liquor. I had had a little vodka before, but not as much as the fifth of Yukon Jack which I drank yesterday. Everybody at the party was saying, 'Go! Go! Go!' They wanted me to finish the whole fifth at once.

"I took one shot and my eyes started watering and I was breathing weird. Then I was taking the bottle and pouring the whiskey down my throat. After a while it seemed to go down like water. Kids were even putting ashes in it and trying to light it on fire, and I was still drinking it.

"I felt all right at first, but then I began to get dizzy and started vomiting. I felt pretty bad after that and was staggering and falling into people, walls, and chairs. It wasn't fun at all. I finally passed out on the couch.

"That was where I was when somebody pushed me out the door. I said to myself, 'Hell with it. You either walk down the hill or fall down the hill.'

"All I was worried about was getting home—and falling. I was scared because I barely knew where I was. All I had to do was to walk a straight line from where I was to Main Street; and I forgot where I was going. I would get to a corner and wonder, 'Which way do I have to go?'

"I passed out in front of an insurance agency. The cops picked me up there. It was freaky. I had three cops standing over me saying, 'Where were you?, Where were you?' with me saying, 'Can't tell ya.' I knew I was in trouble. You don't go to the police station if you are not in trouble.

"I don't know where I was once I was in the station—out behind the dispatcher, I think. I was sitting toppled over in the chair. They asked me who I was; I could hardly remember.

"The police filed a report on me. They could bring me to court, but they won't because it was my first offense. I will have to serve community time and they want me to go to counseling.

"My parents came and got me at the police station. They grounded me for two weeks. Once I got home I slept for twelve and a half hours. I don't think they like me much for what I did.

"The whole school knows about it now. I haven't had this much attention before. I'm kind of a celebrity in school. A lot of kids say, 'That was great yesterday, what you did.' I don't like that; I could have been killed.

"You know, at the party there were two girls and forty guys.

The girls were trying to help me. But a couple of my friends who were supposed to watch me left without me. Somebody could have given me a ride, but they didn't, and that was really not fair. I guess they didn't care enough about me to take care of me.

"I know that I will not get drunk again. It's not worth it. I can picture myself going out again in two months having a couple of drinks. But I will never get that drunk again."

If you do decide to get drunk it will be good for you to go through the hangover: the headaches, the vomiting, the muscle aches, and the saggy eyeballs. It is a good lesson in what alcohol can do.

But instead of risking your life, it would be better if you knew what alcohol would do to you, both physically and psychologically, when taken in different amounts before you drink it.

What Kind of an Effect?

What kind of effect a set amount of alcohol will have on you will depend on:

Your weight
Your age
How often you drink
How fast you drink
How much food you have in your stomach when you drink

For example, let's say that you weigh 120 pounds and you have a friend who weighs the same. If you drink one drink in two hours (a drink is anything with one ounce of alcohol in it; a can of beer has about one ounce, a six-ounce glass of wine has about one ounce, and a one-ounce glass of whiskey, gin, or vodka has one ounce), you won't be as drunk as your friend who had two drinks in one hour.

If you have just eaten and your friend hasn't, the effect on him or her will be even greater compared to the effect on you. The food in your stomach will act like a sponge and will slow the speed at which the alcohol enters your blood and gets to your brain. Also, if you have drank before and your friend hasn't you will be more likely to stay in control longer.

There is a lot of information available about how alcohol will affect you. As Kristin Rancourt said, "it is easy to get if you want it (and you should want it). Go to a police station, a counseling center, a hospital, or call your doctor or ask your parent."

The other thing you can do is to get a Drink/Drive Calculator, which can show you just how much alcohol you can drink in an hour to reach a certain effect. It will show you when the amount of alcohol you have in you is dangerous, and it also shows just how long it takes for you to get undrunk or for the alcohol to leave your system.

One problem with the calculator for teenagers is that it really looks like it is designed for adults. What this means is that even if you weigh as much as an adult you will not be as used to drinking as adults are and so the effect will be much greater on you, even if you drink the same amount of alcohol. It will help you to avoid drinking so much that you risk going into a coma though.

Maybe the safe thing for us to say is if you are going to drink, be safe. Take your time drinking. But an even safer thing we want to say is, why bother with alcohol at all?

You Can Choose Not to Drink

Not all kids drink. Some don't because maybe one time in their lives they took a sip and they didn't like it. Other kids don't drink because they don't want to get into big fights and car accidents; they may have drunk before and gotten into trouble from it and now know that they cannot handle it very well. They know that it causes pain.

Then there are those kids who really hate alcohol because of what has happened in their lives from the abuse of alcohol by someone in their family. A lot of these kids choose not to drink. They know too many people with drinking problems, and they know that alcohol can turn them into people they can't trust.

When you are going into the seventh grade, you hear things like, "You are going to get offered alcohol in the hallways." Sometimes you do and sometimes you don't. The important thing you should know is that there are kids who don't drink whether they have been offered it or not.

Kathy is a sixteen-year-old girl who is in high school and who doesn't drink. She talked to us about what it feels like not to drink when so many of her classmates do. These are her thoughts:

"I am sixteen and I am in the eleventh grade. I don't drink and I have never been drunk before.

"Seeing the movies and programs on television about alcohol has helped me to make this decision, but mostly I've seen kids in my school who are so out of control. They get shaky from drinking, and I would never want to be like that.

"The other thing that has been important to me is that the drinking seems to cause a lot of problems for kids. Emotionally, I think that as much as they don't want to admit it, it does hurt them a lot. If they drink on school nights I hear a lot of kids coming to school the next day complaining about hangovers, feeling sick and having trouble concentrating on their work. Usually after they have been drinking they are ill. From what I've heard they get really sick and stuff. Some get very depressed. I think that the drinking affects their values, too. I think that if kids drink heavily, they may think it is the only thing life has to offer. It is funny but a lot of kids think that alcohol won't get them in trouble at all. They seem to have an 'it will never happen to me' attitude about it, which I can't understand because there have been so many kids having car accidents and other problems.

"I think you can go to a dance without drinking and have just as much fun as if you do drink. Maybe even more, because when you are drinking you are usually tripping all over yourself. I think that, most of the time, you kind of regret what you did when you were drunk. You either don't remember what happened at all or you find out you made such a fool of yourself that you don't want to show your face in school.

"Probably the best thing about the book you are doing is putting in this viewpoint for kids to read. I think that a lot of the kids in high school think that if they don't drink they're not going to fit in and they won't have any friends.

"My point is that if you don't drink, you might realize that you will have more friends in a way. There are a number of other people I know who have decided not to drink whether there is peer pressure or not because they believe it is going to ruin their lives.

"Plus it is much easier not to start drinking than it is to stop. If kids have been drinking heavily and then stop for a while they are very insecure because of the peer pressure. Once they have been involved with alcohol, the group will be offering them drinks and they will be trying to break away. It makes it hard on them, and they will probably lose a lot of friends in the process.

"That is a pretty painful situation, one that would be nice to avoid."

We think it is good to remember that drinking alcohol is a choice. And you can also make the choice not to drink. What we mean is that if you can say no to alcohol and drugs as a teenager, many of your problems may be solved before they start. Problems like car accidents, and getting caught by your school or the police.

Alcohol and Death

"I had a great time. Thanks for inviting me," said Raquel.

"Are you sure you're okay to drive home?" asked Emily.

"Sure. What's a couple of drinks?" replied Raquel.

Next day in school, Raquel was not there.

"Do you know where Raquel is?" asked Emily.

"Probably has a hangover," said Beth, just joking.

"Hey, let's listen to some music!"

"Now it is time for the local news," said the announcer. "Last night, while driving on Elm Street, a sixteen-year-old girl fell asleep and struck a truck head-on. She was pronounced dead on the scene."

"Oh my, how awful!" said Emily.

The announcer continued, "The girl was later identified as Raquel Smith."

Kerry Loy, a student in our grade, created this story for us. In the TV and radio news and the newspapers, though, we have seen stories about real accidents caused by teenage alcohol abuse. Usually some guy or girl is drunk and is trying to drive home and ends up hitting a bridge or something like that. When kids get into accidents it tears families apart.

Two of us interviewed Mrs. Betty Beal, whose daughter was killed by a drunken driver six years ago. The man who was driving fled the scene of the accident, leaving his drunken brother in the car. He was found and arrested six months later.

She can talk about her daughter's death now. In the interview with Mrs. Beal we learned and felt how much an accident like this affects a family. As she told us about it we felt sad and scared. It was almost as if it was happening right in front of our eyes.

On December 16, 1979, Mrs. Beal's twenty-two-year-old daughter Cynthia was driving her friend to Williams College, in Williamstown, Massachusetts. As they were driving through Pownal, Vermont, they met a car on a curve. The car they met missed the curve and drove into Cynthia's car. Her door was pushed into her, killing her instantly. Her friend, the passenger, was not injured.

This accident took a young girl from her family, and from her life. On the day that this accident happened, Cynthia had been celebrating her brother's sixteenth birthday. This now means that every year when her family celebrates his birthday, they will be facing the day that his oldest sister was killed.

We think that you should know that these tragic things can happen—to anyone, but especially to teenagers because of how little alcohol it takes to mess up your judgment! In fact, we think that the accidents should be shown to kids to let them know what can happen while drinking and driving, that they are real, not made up.

Getting Caught

Every kid who drinks doesn't get caught, but if you decide to drink you take the chance that you will. Most kids who get into trouble get caught at school or by the police. This is a painful thing to happen.

We wondered about what happens when kids get caught drinking in school, and what it is like for kids and their parents. We interviewed the vice-principal of our school, Mr. Krulikowski, to get an idea:

Us: How do teachers react when they find that a student is drinking?

Him: They get very sad. Real sad and real concerned. It even frightens a lot of teachers, because, believe me, mostly teachers are concerned about you and they hate to see you doing any harm to yourself. Whenever we have a drinking incident and they are aware of it, they want to know what is going on and what is being done to help that particular student.

Us: When you find that someone has been drinking before school, do you feel bad?

Him: Yeah. I am concerned that somebody has the need to drink to come to school. I am not sure whether they need to feel good before they come here or that it is so bad that they don't want to be here, so they drink. I don't know whether they want to show off, and that is sad, too. If they have to be proud of coming to school after having been drinking, it makes me feel bad.

I also don't like having to call parents saying, "Please come to school right away, your son or your daughter has been drinking." That hits like a bombshell to a parent. There is always silence on the other end of the phone. It takes about thirty seconds to recover. Then they come whipping down here as fast as they can. It is a mess, there is a lot of tears, a lot of tears on both sides, kids and parents, mothers and fathers. I have had both crying badly. It is not a happy situation.

Us: Would you say that most of the kids who have brought alcohol to school have had trouble at home?

Him: I see that there is a breakdown of communication between parents and kids. I've only had two parents so far who really gave me a hard time about it, who denied the whole thing, who said I was out to get their kid, and who said that I was making a big deal out of nothing. The rest said they were very concerned and very glad they had someone to talk to.

Officer Briggs explained to us what happens when you get caught by the police:

"We have a way of testing to see if a person is intoxicated. There are two things that are used to do the test. One thing is kind of exciting. It is called an Alcosensor. It is a little box that looks like a calculator and has a little tube on the top of it.

"We ask the person to blow into this little tube, and when they do we get an automatic reading that will tell us what percentage of alcohol is in the person's bloodstream. If the number is high enough and if the person is showing other characteristics of drinking—such as slurred speech, watery bloodshot eyes, a strong odor of intoxicating beverages on their breath, or if they have been swerving on the road—then we take them to the station.

"There are a number of punishments that result from drinking. If you are driving you risk loss of your license and fines. The punishments depend on how many times you get caught. A lot, maybe eighty percent, of the people that we arrest at night—especially for crimes such as vandalism, hit-and-run accidents, assaults, and fighting—involve alcohol.

"I've personally arrested one hundred people in our town for drinking and driving. We arrest altogether probably two hundred people a year for drunk driving. In 1972 the police department arrested about thirty people. You can see where enforcement has really taken hold. When I first came on the police department, you would just say, 'Well why don't you push over and let me drive you home?' You kept giving them breaks. I don't think anyone gets taken home anymore. Whether it's a big shot in town or a low-income person, young or old, they are all treated the same. They are all charged."

If Your Drinking Gets Out of Control

If you are getting drunk often and getting yourself in trouble, it means that you are trying to hide some problems; maybe you have gotten dumped by a girlfriend or boyfriend, or maybe you have been beaten up.

If you are drinking all the time, maybe you are worried about problems with your parents. Maybe you are afraid that they are going to get a divorce and you have to decide which parent to live with.

Many kids get depressed because their parents don't care enough about them, so they go drinking to try to get their parents' attention. They will do anything to get their parents to punish them just so that they know their parents care about them.

You should really try to find out why you are getting drunk so often, because kids don't drink all the time without having something bothering them. You are no different.

If your parents catch you drinking or drunk, they will naturally be mad at first. We think that this is good, because you will learn a lesson from the anger and maybe the lesson will be that they care. Maybe your parents won't blow it out of proportion and they will sit down and talk it over with you when you are sober, not when you are drunk. If they get too mad at you, it will only make it worse. Hopefully they will know that scare tactics don't work with kids. It just makes them want to get back at parents for getting so mad.

Remember, too, you may have parents who drink constantly and are bad examples for you and that is why you are having such a hard time. If this is true and your parents find out that you are drinking and then yell at you, they may be yelling at you for doing something they actually taught you to do in the first place. This will mean that the problem is not only you.

The Best Place to Learn to Drink

You can avoid some of the problems that teen drinking brings if you learn to drink from your parents (unless one of them is alcoholic of course).

As you really start to think about alcohol you should sit down and ask your parent about it. You should say, "Mom, tell me about what it is like to drink." It might sound dumb to your parent. He or she might say, "Why are you asking me? You're too young."

This is true, but we think that parents should teach kids how to control themselves when using alcohol anyway. Danny said, "If I had kids who wanted to know how to drink, I would show them the proper way. I'd give them beer and teach them to have a good time and how not to abuse it. I would let them drink it at home and not out in public. I would keep an eye on what they were doing and how they were reacting."

A lot of times parents don't think that their kids are thinking about alcohol. Kids are naturally curious about it. They wonder things like, "What things can go wrong?" "What does it feel like to get drunk?" "What do you see when you get drunk?" "Do you see pink elephants, do you hear bells?" They really are curious and want to know this stuff.

If your parents understand this and are having you drink in a controlled way, you will at least learn how to drink responsibly. Then you won't be so curious about alcohol when you get out with your friends. You may not feel the need to prove yourself.

If you are determined to experience getting drunk, you should just ask your parent to let you try getting drunk at home. Your parent might say to you, "Excuse me, what did you say?" But most parents would understand, because they were kids once, too, and probably felt the same way you do. At least if you get drunk with your parent, you will be safe.

SADD

Being safe when you are a teenage drinker is what is most important.

A thirteen-year-old girl named Michelle said, "My friend's sister is in the hospital. She skipped school and went out with her friends drinking and got badly hurt in a car accident. My mom said to me that if I was ever with anybody and was drinking, she wouldn't get mad if I called home for a ride."

This is the Contract for Life. It is produced by the Students Against Driving Drunk. It is an agreement between you and your parents that no matter what the situation, if you are drunk or need a ride home from a party, they will come get you—no questions asked.

We would all sign a Contract for Life because if we ever do

want to go out drinking, we might want and be assured there is a safe way home.

We think, however, that there are some problems with the contract. One is that kids are often too drunk to call home. Since they are so drunk, they get scared that their parents are going to get mad at them.

We also don't think that every parent would keep his or her end of the deal. Some parents wouldn't wait until the kids had some sleep before they got angry. Nevertheless, we still think that you should have your parent come and get you. It's better than getting into a car with a drunk driver. Wouldn't you would rather be yelled at the next morning than be dead?

The parents who would sign this contract are parents who are not alcoholic. If one of your parents is an alcoholic, this contract could be signed, but you run the risk that your parent is drinking at home while you are out. If that is true, what is the sense of calling? You could have just as easily ridden home with another drunk.

You should only call your parents if you are sure that they are not going to be drunk when you call. If they are drunk, you could think about calling a relative or a friend who you know can pick you up. You can maybe call a grandparent, or an aunt or uncle. We could redesign this form to call it the Contract for Life for Kids Without Alcoholic Parents, but we think it is good enough already.

Another problem is that alcoholic kids aren't going to sign this. They are not going to want to admit to their parents that they have alcohol problems. This is because if you are alcoholic, you don't really care what happens when you are drinking. We are not sure that there is such a thing as a responsible alcoholic.

Some kids, believe it or not, would not sign the Contract for Life because they think that it is babyish. They might be afraid that their friends think it is silly.

Some of us plan on never drinking, but we would sign it anyway, just in case some kid would call us "chickens" and then we might just decide to get drunk. We would have a way to get home.

Even though you may say now that you are not going to drink when you get older (or right now), there is a chance that you could. You just never know.

The Drinking Age

Some of your parents might be strict and not let you drink even at home until you reach the legal drinking age. They may be afraid that it will influence you to drink even more than you would usually be influenced.

There are many different opinions about what the drinking age should be, and you should know them. These are some of them:

Mr. Michael Mahar, a bartender and restaurant operator: "I am a liberal. I don't think that it is fair to ask people to be responsible as citizens at the age of eighteen and not allow them to drink. The way to relieve the drinking problem is through education in the school and not through legislation in general.

"Whatever age it is in one state it should be in all states. There are other people who have the opinion that the age should be twenty-one. Perhaps they are right, but I just don't happen to feel that way. You can't give somebody something and then take it away. What I am against is trying to legislate more and more laws. We can't enforce the laws that we have."

Police Officer Gary Briggs: "The drinking age should be twenty-one, no questions asked. A lot of people are still immature at eighteen. A good share of the people that we pick up are between the ages of eighteen and twenty-one. A lot of the fatalities that happen are by people between eighteen and twenty-one who have been drinking."

Mr. Anthony Krulikowski, vice-principal: "When I was eighteen, I wished it were eighteen. Now that I am forty I wish it were twenty-one. When I was growing up, the drinking age was twenty-one. We drank before that, but I was glad it was twenty-one. I felt like a big deal, drinking legally at twenty-one. I wouldn't have felt that way at eighteen. Eighteen-year-olds should be allowed to vote, but they shouldn't be allowed to drink. They are not fully grown.

"It seems that now that the drinking age is eighteen, people are drinking younger, people in your age group are drinking. When I was growing up, I didn't know of anybody who was going out and getting drunk at twelve, thirteen, and so on. It just wasn't available for that kind of thing, and that is scary.

"Yes, it is like getting a driver's license. Waiting until you are sixteen helps. Just because you are a human being, you don't have the same rights that adults have. You don't have the same rights that we have. You have to earn those things, you have to show responsibility."

Mr. Ronald Knapp, Vermont state legislator: "The drinking age needs to be raised. Alcohol does one thing that is very bad: It tends to make us think we are making good decisions, but we aren't even able to make as good a decision as we are when we are not drinking. The more alcohol we have, the greater we think we are, but the poorer our judgment is. For that reason I would like to see the drinking age raised. When we make bad decisions like that we can kill ourselves, kill our friends, and kill innocent people on the highway.

"Another reason it is important to raise the age is that at this point in time we are surrounded by states with drinking ages higher than Vermont. This means that young folks from those states come into Vermont in substantial numbers and are drinking and then driving back home.

"There has been talk about if the drinking age is higher than the age to be drafted, why should people have to go into the army if they can't drink? That is a real good question that has been debated a lot since I was a state representative and has been debated a lot even before that. I think that if people my age who make the laws had to go out and fight, they probably wouldn't be the same kind of fighters as our younger people. We have different and more mature judgment and we would be more careful, a little more reserved and a little less willing to take commands.

"It is important to have people in our armed forces who will take commands and act instantly. They don't have the experience to make good judgments all the time. Young people do well in the armed forces and do the job that needs to be done, but when you take a young person whose judgment is not yet mature to consume alcohol and other drugs, you reduce his ability to make good judgments. When you do that you have a less effective and a less valuable soldier. So I don't think you really can equate the right to drink.

"When something impairs your judgment, it is not a right, it is a privilege."

Paul M., recovering alcoholic: "For a drinking age, forty-five would be good; I am serious, I am radical. I think it should have stayed where it was. There is a big difference between eighteen and twenty-one."

Judy S., recovering alcoholic: "The drinking age should be twenty-one, definitely. When people reach the age of twenty-one they are more mature. Before, when they had the drinking age at eighteen, a lot of kids looked like they were eighteen when they were really only sixteen or seventeen. They could go in and get served. But when you reach the age of twenty-one you start to look more like you are then when you were fifteen or sixteen years old."

Mark C., recovering alcoholic: "The drinking age should be eighteen. Rather than making a legal argument out of it, we should make a social argument out of it. We should educate our children on the hazards of becoming too involved in alcohol and drugs. When I was drinking, the age was twenty-one. It didn't make a difference. You were an adult if you smoked, you were an adult if you drank, and you were an adult if you had sex. As a kid under twenty-one, I mimicked the adult world that I saw."

Kathy W., high school student: "The drinking age should be twenty-one. Kids at eighteen still can't control alcohol. I know a girl who had a drug overdose. It was caused by alcohol. She got to the point where she had problems at home and school and it just got too much for her. There was another guy I know who was drunk and was riding on a motorcycle and got killed. A lot of kids think that 'it will never happen to me,' but there have been so many car accidents and some kids at school have been in car accidents that I don't know how they could think that."

Janie D., high school student: "Maybe if the drinking age was twenty-one kids won't cause so many deaths on the highway. Alcohol is going to come at you when you are at a very young age. I was exposed to it when I was in the seventh grade. It doesn't matter how old you are, you are still going to be exposed to it. You are still going to have to make a decision sooner or later whether you want to drink or whether you don't want to drink. So I really don't think that a drinking age will make that much of a difference."

Jim P., high school student: "The drinking age should be eighteen . . . definitely. A lot of eighteen-year-olds are responsible as far as drinking goes. Kids under eighteen drink more than kids over eighteen do. Seriously. No matter if they raise the drinking age to twenty-eight, people are still going to get it. If they can't buy it, they will steal it. I know a lot of kids who steal it."

To us, the drinking age doesn't make that much difference. We think that the drinking age should be twenty-one, and we agree with Mr. Krulikowski, who said that kids should earn the right to drink. But we know that what Jim P. says is true: If kids want alcohol, they will get it.

If You Wait, You Might Find You Don't Need Alcohol

Nonetheless, some of us think kids should wait to begin to drink until they have reached the drinking age, because if they do they might not want to drink at all. They might say to themselves, "Hey, I lived through life until now not drinking, why can't I still do it?"

Just because you have the right to drink doesn't mean you have to. Other people might feel different, but that is the way we feel. There is nothing magical about drinking. It can be fun to drink, but it depends on where you are and who you are with. If you are at home and you have a party with your parents, that can be fun. It can mean you are starting to be grown up. You can say to yourself, "I must be starting to be mature, because my parents are letting me do more things."

Alcohol isn't everything. You can make the choice to not drink. And if you don't drink, you don't ever have to worry about becoming alcoholic, which, if you have grown up in an alcoholic family, is a real possibility for you.

Chapter IV

Alcoholism

"I liked the thrill of the alcohol when I started to drink. It was a challenge, to my friend and me, to see if we could handle the things that the adults did. It was kind of an adventure to get my mother's brandy bottle out and drink some, between the house and the church next to us, to see what it did. There is a Chinese saying: 'The man takes a drink, the drink takes a drink, then the drink takes the man.' If you get into enough trouble with alcohol, you don't have control over yourself; you become physically and psychologically addicted."   Mark C., recovering alcoholic

When we hear the word "alcoholism" we think:

Danger
Murder
Poison ivy in a rose garden
A wolf in sheep's clothing

Alcoholism is a disease that can destroy your body, your mind, and your family. We think of it as an error in some human beings that causes problems in their judgment regarding the substance called alcohol. In other words, it causes them to become addicted to alcohol. We picture an alcoholic as steel and alcohol as a magnet.

This picture doesn't look good to us and makes us sad. We feel sorry for people who have problems with alcohol, because while writing this book we have learned what alcoholism can do to people. Some of us know about alcoholism from living with alcoholics: aunts, uncles, brothers, cousins, grandparents, mothers and fathers.

Anyone Can Become Alcoholic

Anyone can be an alcoholic and anyone can become alcoholic. People you may have known for years may be alcoholics without you knowing it. Because alcoholism is not limited by characteristics of any sort, the people we are talking about could be friends and relatives of either sex, any race, and any age.

For example, Bob S. is only seventeen and is a recovering alcoholic:

"I live with my mother and have four younger brothers. I met my father once when I was thirteen years old; my father was alcoholic. I started drinking because I was really hurting inside and I was looking for an escape from the problems I was hurting from.

"One of my earliest memories is my grandfather being drunk and my mother taking him to a bowling alley to get my uncle, who was also drunk. I was only five at the time. When we got to the bowling alley my grandfather climbed out of the car and beat up my uncle for being drunk.

"It was real sick. There were all these people standing around watching this go on. Since it was his son, they thought they couldn't do anything. For me, it was real painful. I would go up to my grandfather and say, 'Stop hitting him. Leave him alone, leave him alone!'

"Because my father was not in my life, I was sad. If I was playing football, or whatever I was doing, I knew that he was not there to watch me, or to say, 'Way to go, son.' When I got to be a teenager, I would see people laughing and having a good time while drinking beer and smoking pot; I had seen my mother, my father, and my stepfather smoking pot, and I figured that it must work. So I tried it, but it didn't work and it was painful. Luckily, I learned a lot from it."

The Right Mix

Things like too much stress caused by everyday affairs, not being educated about the effects of alcohol, or maybe a death in the family can make addiction to alcohol more of a possibility for someone. Judy S., a recovering alcoholic, said, "When I really started drinking was after my husband was killed in a motorcycle accident. I was pregnant at the time with my youngest one. My friends came to the house and wanted me to go out with them to bars. They said I didn't have to drink, but going out would help me to enjoy myself."

It does seem that whether people become addicted to alcohol or not depends upon their genes, their personalities, and their histories.

A gene, according to the Grolier International Dictionary, is a functional hereditary unit. For example, you have a gene in your body for hair color. The gene gets passed from one of your parents to you. What that means is if your parent has brown hair you have a good chance of having brown hair, too. Alcoholism works somewhat in the same way.

Alcoholism might be passed to people through their genes. Dan heard on the radio that a Canadian doctor has found that alcoholism is transported in this way. That means if your father is alcoholic, you have more of a chance of becoming an alcoholic because it is inherent in your body structure.

Of course, you might have the gene inside you to become alcoholic but you might not like alcoholic beverages, so that would keep you from being alcoholic. Or, as Shane Squiers suggested, "Maybe you understand the problem and what it would do to you, so you don't want to drink." Understanding can be a powerful force to avoid alcoholism, because people can only become alcoholic by drinking.

David O'Brien, a substance abuse specialist, told us that some people are "allergic" to alcohol. He said, "Some of you might be allergic to things like cats, dogs, dust, or whatever. That means your bodies don't like you to be around them and you probably don't have any problems until you get around those things. It is the same with alcohol. If you are allergic to it, all you have to do is start drinking it and then you are going to have problems with it."

It is sort of like Gwen Shorey imagined, a puzzle. "If you have the gene, you have one piece. If you add on a certain history and personality, then it keeps just building up until somebody says to you, 'Hey, you need help.' "

Mark C. told us that he didn't know whether he had the genes of addiction to alcohol, but he did know that he had the history and the personality. He said, "There are a lot of alcoholics in my family. My grandfather on my mother's side of the family was alcoholic. I am sure there were some drunks on my father's side of the family. I have not found out about them yet, but the patterns in that part of the family are the same as in the other. I learned to not feel by drinking. I learned, by watching other people drinking, that I could blot out everything.

"Most alcoholics have compulsive personalities. What that means is if something tastes good, the alcoholic will eat the whole pot. If one beer tastes good, then two have got to taste better. For example, I am a diabetic. If I have a reaction and need to eat something sweet and I come up upon fourteen candy bars or cookies, I will eat them all."

So if a person has the right mix of genes, history, and personality, and then he or she drinks and drinks and drinks, his or her body will create a craving for alcohol.

Alcoholism or Alcohol Abuse?

It can be hard to understand just who is alcoholic and who isn't. For example, there are people who abuse alcohol who may look alcoholic but are drinking heavily as a result of momentary stress. One girl told us, "Right before my mom and dad got divorced, when they were fighting a lot and everything, my dad used to go out and drink. He didn't go out and get drunk all the time, though once in a while he would go out and get very drunk, but he barely drinks now."

He was a problem drinker. There is a difference between problem drinking and alcoholism, the biggest difference being that problem drinkers usually bring an end to their drinking when the problem is over, while the alcoholic continues to drink on forever.

How do you decide what alcoholism is and what it isn't? Another girl told us that her uncle could drink two six-packs of beer and not get drunk. Is he alcoholic? He could be. We wondered whether a person who has two drinks a day, forever, is alcoholic. It is possible. Then we questioned whether someone could drink five drinks a day and *not* be alcoholic. We guessed that this person would definitely be alcoholic.

We talked about this a lot, and it became very confusing.

This is a discussion that we had in trying to decide what alcoholism is:

Kim W.: Do you think that to be an alcoholic you have to drink all the time?

Dan: You can drink occasionally and still be an alcoholic. It is that you don't have any control over how much you drink when you do drink.

Kim W.: So you can drink a little of the time and be alcoholic?

Dan: Yes, if you overindulge when you drink.

Kim W.: Do you think, and I am talking to everyone here, that you can drink one beer every night at the same time and be an alcoholic?

Meg: Yes.

Jason R.: It doesn't matter how much you drink or when you started drinking. If you start drinking at all you are an alcoholic, no matter if you have only one or two every night.

Tammy: Yes, if you drink one every night, pretty soon after a year or so, if you get into it, you will just drink more and more, so you become addicted to it.

Kim W.: So you think that people just become addicted, that no matter what, it is just going to build up? There is someone who said no. Let's get your opinion on this. If you drink one beer at the same time every night, would you be an alcoholic?

Mike: No! I know lots of people who drink a beer every night and watch television or whatever. Alcoholism is a disease. You can drink a little bit each night and it doesn't mean you will become alcoholic.

Meg: It could go either way. A person who is an alcoholic could drink every now and then and be an alcoholic, or a person can drink a lot and not be an alcoholic.

Kim W.: So alcoholism depends on the person. You can have one person who gets bombed once a year and isn't an alcoholic but have another person who gets blasted once a year and is. It has to depend on the person. Is it an individual thing, then?

Say if someone can drink and drink and they can just stop whenever they want to, compared with someone who can just drink and drink and drink and can't stop. Which one is the alcoholic?

Gwen: The one who can't stop.

If someone drinks alcohol, he or she is not necessarily an alcoholic. If someone gets drunk once in his or her life, it doesn't mean alcoholism. There are, in fact, people who have gotten drunk plenty of times and have not ended up addicted to alcohol. If you can drink and control it, then you are not alcoholic.

It is confusing. But think of it as Mike Mahar, one of the authors, did. "Alcoholism," he said, "is a disease. Alcohol abuse is not a disease. Abusing alcohol is more your choice, but abusing alcohol because of alcoholism is more the alcohol's choice."

Alcoholism Is a Progressive Disease

Alcoholism is a progressive disease. What this means is that if people you care about are alcoholic, they will get gradually worse over time. They could progress from being drunk once in a while to every night and, sometimes, to being drunk most of the time.

The stages of drinking in alcoholism usually progress something like this:

In the Beginning drinking is:

Fun
Exciting
Great

In the Middle the alcoholic may:

Have many drinks
Get drunk a lot
Want to stop drinking but not be able to

In the End the alcoholic may:

Try to quit before dying
Not be able to quit and die
Be getting help

If people have the disease of alcoholism they will never get rid of it. They can stop drinking, but they don't stop being alcoholic. It isn't that the alcohol is still in their system; in fact, they may not ever get drunk again. It is that one drink will cause them to want more. Judy S. said, "Even though I only occasionally have a drink now, as soon as I take that first drink, it would be very easy for me to keep right on drinking." And Mark C. said, "I can't even allow myself to drink nonalcoholic substitutes. I thought about it once but realized that when I drank, I drank to get drunk, not for the taste. I am afraid if I drank the nonalcoholic beer it would be just too easy for me to go to the real thing."

The time that it takes each person to go through the process of alcoholism varies. Some alcoholics have no control over their drinking from their first drink on. They start each of their days off with beer and then drink more and more as the days go on. Others start slowly and limit themselves, at times, to a few drinks.

David O'Brien told us that he has seen sixteen-year-olds who were in the late stages of alcoholic drinking and older people who were just in the beginning stages. To us, it is like having two race-car drivers driving identical cars in a big race. One goes two hundred miles and crashes; the other one goes much farther before wiping out. That is the same way it is for alcoholics.

Signs of Alcoholism

All alcoholics are not alike. Some alcoholics are sneaky. Some bum around and don't care about their kids, while others do the exact opposite. One boy said, "My uncle Henry has a problem with alcohol, but he still is a caring parent."

When they are drunk, not all alcoholics act alike. They can be:

Silly
Calm
Delirious
Violent
Abusive

There *are* some things that can cause you to suspect people in your life to be alcoholic, though.

Their Drinking: When alcoholics drink, they drink frantically, usually, as someone said, "until their eyes pop out." Judy S. said, "I took the second job just to supply my habit. When I'd get through work I would just sit there until closing time and drink. I spent more money than what I was making. I was only going one night a week and drinking. Mainly when I was doing that it was because I was lonely and needed some time out away from the kids. On these Saturday nights I just couldn't begin to keep track on how much I did drink."

Mark C. said, "In my earlier days, I would drink two six-packs a day. By the end of my drinking I was drinking two fifths of whiskey a day on the weekends plus four six-packs each day. I got to the point where I would drink anything with alcohol. I had a friend whose parents made home brew in a crock pot. It used to be so strong that it blew the bottoms out of the bottles. We drank it anyway."

Their Bodies: Dr. Loy described to us reactions of the body that he pays attention to in finding out whether someone has problems with alcohol. He said, "One effect that I can think of is the red nose that people who drink a lot of alcohol develop. Their blood vessels stay open so much because of the alcohol in their system that their vessels break just under the skin. When I see broken blood vessels in the nose or around the cheeks I start to wonder if the person isn't using too much alcohol."

Alcoholics do damage to their bodies in other ways, too. Some of the damage is self-inflicted, like when they get so drunk that they cut their fingers while cutting tomatoes or something, without feeling a thing. Some get so drunk that they fall on their faces or run into doors and break their noses.

Their Emotions: An important way to tell if someone close to you has a problem with alcohol is if his or her personality changes after drinking alcohol. Alcoholics live in two different worlds. There is the good world when they are sober and being themselves. When alcoholics get drunk, they go into another world and are like complete different people. They may all of a sudden be mean, sad, or depressed.

> Let's say you meet someone. When you first know this person, he or she is really nice, really loving and caring; so you marry the person. Then whenever he or she drinks, violence and abusiveness begins.
>
> Your favorite uncle is always nice to you, takes you places and everything, but when he drinks, he may not care for you as much.
>
> Your parent is nice during the day but then goes to a party, starts drinking right away, and drinks all through the night until the party is over. Then he or she comes home and starts yelling at you.

Those are all kinds of personality changes and are possible signs of alcoholism.

Their Memories: Blackouts are one of the most important signs of alcoholism. Blackouts come, according to Dr. Loy, because "alcoholism is a big strain on the brain and can cause the brain, in alcoholics, to stop functioning. It can get so bad that if an alcoholic drinks for too long, he or she will eventually not be able to remember things that happened even when not drinking."

Mark C. told us about his blackouts. "Blackouts are doing

things and not remembering them until someone tells you. I remember a time when I was enrolled in some technical courses. I would have a class in the evening that would let out at nine o'clock. After class I would have to drive twenty-five miles to my house and arrive home around a quarter to ten. I would drink six beers in the twenty-five-mile space and not remember the drive home at all.

"Another time I must have backed into my father's porch and knocked it right off the side of the house. I didn't realize it until the next day when I saw the leftover pile of lumber in the yard. I asked, 'What jerk ran over that?' He said, 'You!' "

Their Actions: Alcoholics will often get themselves into trouble from drinking. Mark C. said, "When I was younger, as a teenager, a friend of mine and I went out drinking and riding around. Somewhere along the road we passed the commissioner of motor vehicles and the head of the state police. We were going a little bit faster than we should have been and they threw us in jail. When I was sixteen or seventeen, my friend and I were drinking while we were talking on the phone. It was possible to talk from a phone by driving a car close to the booth. At some point while I was talking he drove off. When he drove away I still had the receiver in my hand. I had pulled it right off. We thought that was kind of funny. So we went all the way to the Canadian border pulling out phones like that. That got us in a little trouble, too."

Another kind of trouble alcoholics get themselves into is fights. Judy S. said, "I was working at a bar once where the owner was an alcoholic who was dating a married woman who lived up the street. She stormed into the bar one night and accused me of going out with my boss. I grabbed hold of her and went out in the parking lot. She and I had a knockdown, drag-out fight. I was so drunk that I didn't know that I had been fighting until people told me about it the next day. I said, 'I did that?' It was a wonder that she didn't knock the daylights out of me. I got the best of her, and honestly, I don't know how."

Many alcoholics do things to risk their jobs. They go to work sometimes really drunk or hung over. Judy S. said, "When I was drinking heavily, I was a short-order cook in a diner; the job was very demanding. I would go in with a hangover and it was pretty rough. I managed to pull through it; I guess my boss didn't realize I was suffering from a hangover—but I was."

Their Disasters: Many alcoholics fall asleep on the highway. Keith Thompson, a thirteen-year-old we interviewed, said, "My stepfather fell asleep at the wheel after drinking and took down seven guardrails with his car. Then the police came to our house to find him."

Bob S. told us, "When I was drinking, my whole thought process was thrown out of whack. It was like the Twilight Zone. Most of the time I was kind of crazy and off the wall. There was one time at a skating rink, I think I was in the tenth grade, that I got really blitzed. We were at war with another group of kids over some foolishness—I think we had thrown some crab apples at their cars or something. When you are at this age, things like that upset you. So this kid came out of the rink and pushed one of us. I decided to take him on.

"I had these stitches in my arm because one of my good friends, good drinking buddies, threw a knife at me. When I went to fight this kid, I had one of my good drinking buddies cut my stitches out. These are the kind of guys that I used to hang around with when I was drinking. So he took a knife and cut the stitches out and the cut was hanging wide open.

"I guess I went in the roller rink and was chasing the kid around. The policeman in there grabbed me and threw me up against the wall by the hair. He was trying to pull me out of the rink and I was yelling and screaming at him. He finally threw me out, but I ran back in and jumped over the railing onto the skating-rink floor. People were flying everywhere. I became a real legend at the rink for a while."

Their Stoppings: Mark C. said, "I tried quitting all the time and I never could do it. I would always drink. I would say, 'I won't drink until noon.' Then at eleven I would say, 'It's close enough.' If I had one drink, I couldn't stop, I would drink until I passed out, which could be all day, or toward the end, it was like half a day."

Alcoholics stop drinking over and over again. Things like problems in the family or at work cause them to stop for a while. Maybe alcoholics will act stupid or silly and sometimes cry a lot. Maybe they will curse at friends and relatives or even hurt them. After these things happen, friends or relatives may begin to tell them that they drink too much and may even threaten to leave if they don't quit.

When everything has calmed down at home or at work, the alcoholic always starts drinking again. Judy S. said, "When I first started drinking, I got really sick. I drank so much that I would say, 'I'm never going to do that again.' Then Saturday night would come around and I would go out and do it all over. You can't help yourself after you start drinking; it does make you feel on top of the world. Whenever you sober up, you say, 'I'll never do this again,' but then, if you are an alcoholic, you turn right around and do it."

Alcoholics Are Good at Avoiding Being Identified as Alcoholics

The alcoholics you know might act strange. They might stumble often or just not seem like themselves. Maybe their eyes will be bloodshot or their breath will smell like alcohol all the time. Some might act insecure when sober because they think that everyone knows they have been drinking. Too often, though, you can't tell when people around you are alcoholic.

This is because alcoholics are *very good* at avoiding being identified as alcoholic. Alcoholics are simply good liars. They don't tell people when they are drunk, or they try to act cool about it when they are. Some of the alcoholics in your life will say they don't want a drink when someone offers one to them. Some might carry around brown bags with alcohol in them but say that it is only soda. Other things they do to avoid being identified as alcoholics are:

Drink alone
Drink in isolated places
Have someone else buy their liquor
Hide their alcohol

We made up a scene about ways that alcoholics can sneak drinks on the job.

Interviewer: Are you a businessman? If you are a businessman, where do you find time to drink?

Drunk: On the way home, in the car, or I stop on the way home and get drunk.

Interviewer: You stop at a bar on the way home?

Drunk: Yeah, why not? I drink in the office, too.

Interviewer: Where can an alcoholic keep alcohol in an office?

Drunk: In the drawer or the wastebasket. If I have to, I bring a Thermos of orange juice and put some liquor in it. A smart fellow would have a revolving door on the wall with a shelf in it.

Alcoholics do these things for a lot of reasons. Jason Roberts thought of a few. He said, "Some are embarrassed and may feel confused because they can't stop drinking. They know they are alcoholic and don't want to be. Others think their friends won't like them as a result of finding out what they do when they are drunk. Many hide their alcoholism so that friends and relatives won't try to take them to get help."

Most important, alcoholics don't want other people knowing they have a problem with alcohol because they think they can't live without it. Mark C. said, "If I were in a place where I wanted to drink and I wasn't allowed to, I was in trouble. I was very uncomfortable. I used alcohol to buffer my fear of talking to people. If this interview was happening seven or eight years ago, I would have had to have a drink to be able to answer your questions. Alcohol took away my shyness. For example, when I was a younger fellow I was always afraid to ask girls to dance. So I would drink to get up my courage. By the time I had enough to drink to get up my courage, I couldn't walk, and who wants to dance with a babbling drunk?"

A Test

If people in your life do some of these things, you might try to make them aware of problems that, in fact, are major problems. We made up a test to help you show the alcoholic in your life that there is a problem.

1. When you go to a party, is drinking alcohol all that you want to do?
2. Do you have to drink a lot in order to be happy?
3. Do you drink because you have problems?
4. Do you ever have blackouts?
5. Do you drink alcohol to handle your problems at home?
6. Do you have problems at home because of your drinking?
7. Has anyone ever told you that you are an alcoholic?
8. Have you ever tried to sneak alcohol when you are alone?
9. Do you drink alcohol and drive?
10. Do you consider yourself an alcoholic?

If they answer yes to any one of these questions it doesn't mean automatically that they are alcoholic, but it should make them think about themselves and alcohol. The more they answer yes, the more they should think.

Be careful though. It isn't always easy, even with a test, to make an alcoholic aware of the problem, because the world from the eyes of an alcoholic is a real big mess!

Alcoholics really don't like to admit they are alcoholic at all. They *deny* everything. Denial is the refusal to admit the truth of a statement. Say somebody told you that you were alcoholic and you said, "No, I am not. I am a heavy drinker," or you said, "I can stop drinking anytime." These are examples of denial. Alcoholics, because of this attitude, are good at keeping themselves from admitting they have a problem.

Usually, if you try to tell them that they have problems with alcohol, they say things like:

"Everyone drinks."

"Everyone has problems."

"You have a problem."

If that doesn't work, they just won't talk to you about it at all. They cover it up by running away, getting angry, or starting fights. In these ways they can just keep on convincing themselves that it is okay to drink and that they are not alcoholics.

The World from the Eyes of an Alcoholic

Drinking or sober, for the actively drinking alcoholic the world is a bottle of alcohol. Mark C. said, "Toward the last part of my drinking, if I was sent down to the store for a quart of milk, a loaf of bread, and a pound of hamburger, I usually wouldn't bring it back, or if I had it I wouldn't get back until one or two in the morning. I would see a friend at a bar, stop in for one drink. I wouldn't go home unless there was booze there. At five minutes of twelve, when the stores were going to close, I would drive five miles to a store to get a six-pack of beer because I was so afraid of waking up at home with no booze in the house."

Gwen Shorey thought that, "There are some alcoholics who when drinking find the world scary and confusing, a blurry, hard-to-understand place, maybe even as something bad. The world is something against them." For most, though, the drunken, alcoholic world is great, fun, and wonderful. They are having fun and feeling cool. Feeling good about themselves, they act as if they had no problems at all, as if they were the most important ones in the world, or sometimes, the only ones.

Then, when alcoholics are sober, they can be like people without personalities. They can become:

Sorry for themselves

More nervous

Depressed

Harder to talk to

They may feel pretty awful about themselves and wish they didn't drink; they may see themselves as losers. Mark C. said, "I think that I felt ashamed when I was sober. When I was in high school, I was the drunk of my hometown."

Either Way, Families Are a Bother

Either way, alcoholics see their families as being in the way of the bottle. As Mark C. said, "I would more or less push my family in a corner. I was married to my second wife when my drinking was the heaviest. I kept them at a distance, because drinking was the main focus in my life."

Chapter V

Living with
An Alcoholic

If your parents used to be very nice to you,
And active with you,
But now, when they drink,
Scream and holler at you;
Or if they get babysitters
Every night,
Just so they can go out to bars;
Or if one of them hits you
When they drink;
and if and when these things happen
You feel like you don't get enough love and understanding,
They and you are having problems—
With alcohol.

A GROUP POEM

Some kids say that your mother is your most important parent (most kids do spend more time with their mothers than their fathers) and if your mother is the alcoholic in your life, it will be harder on you than if your father is the alcoholic.

Other kids say that if you are a boy in a family and the alcoholic is your father, it will hurt you more; or if you are a girl in a family and the alcoholic is your mother, that this will hurt you more.

If you live in an alcoholic family though, it hurts you one way or the other. You know this, because you *know* some things that other kids don't.

Things You Know

You *know* that alcoholic families are strange and that alcoholism seems to create problems for kids whether the alcoholic parent is drunk or sober.

Typical day: The alcoholic comes home late, usually in a bad mood, and affects everyone in the family: mother or father, sister or brother. The next morning everyone goes where they are supposed to (school or work), except the alcoholic, who is still sleeping. When everyone then comes home, the problems start. Let's say you bring a friend home from school. You are in a very good mood and say, "Hi, Mom, [or Dad]. Guess what? I got an A on a test today." The alcoholic then yells at you for not getting an A+. Next your mother or father comes home and starts arguing with your alcoholic parent. The whole family is now disrupted. You leave with your friend and your day is crashed.

You *know* some crazy things are bound to happen to kids when a parent drinks too much.

Frank Jones, age thirteen, said, "My stepmother starts drinking when she gets up: around six in the morning. She drinks until bedtime: about seven or seven-thirty at night. Sometimes she is happy; sometimes she is mad. She doesn't usually eat supper but will get up in the middle of the night and eat—then leave everything out. One night she broke a jelly jar and left it on the floor where she dropped it. When one of my little sisters got up to go to the bathroom, she cut her foot wide open on the glass. Since the kitchen is right next to my bedroom, I heard her screaming and went to help her; then my dad woke up and washed her foot and we took her to the hospital."

You *know* that if one of your parents is an alcoholic, you miss things that kids in nonalcoholic families don't.

Some of us who have lived in alcoholic families wondered

what it was like not to ever have to deal with the problem of alcoholism. Gwen Shorey, one of the authors, has never had to face it. She said, "My father has a collection of two hundred fifty beer bottles, and occasionally he will find a beer bottle that he doesn't have, but he isn't an alcoholic. My mother is definitely not an alcoholic. She doesn't even like the stuff!

"At our house we do a lot of talking, and together-with-the-family things like camping, fishing, hiking, swimming, and those sorts of things. If I lived in an alcoholic family, I don't think we would do so many together-with-the-family things (which I enjoy), because I have the impression that alcoholics like to be by themselves a lot."

You *know* that if you live in an alcoholic home, you can feel jealousy or even hatred for people who don't, because you don't spend the same kind of time with your family as they do.

From your point of view it is strange, but natural, to have your parent get drunk; you are used to it and learn to expect it. When it happens, you are used to the communication between you and your alcoholic parent getting cut off.

Alcoholic parents hardly ever understand what you say. Take dinnertime, for example. Too often your alcoholic parent (if he or she is there at all) will fall asleep face-first in the food; or if that doesn't happen, when you try to have a conversation, your parent will just keep repeating the same things over and over.

In fact, whenever the alcoholic is home, the whole family balance is thrown off. Things like what you say, when you say it, and how you say it change automatically.

You *know* that alcoholism in one of your parents can cause your relationship to your other parent to change for the worse.

Tom Mitchell, age twelve, said, "Being a kid in an alcoholic family is hard. In my case, my dad is the bad guy even when he is sober because he used to get drunk a lot. My mom tends to force on me what she thinks of my dad and wants me to agree with everything she says or thinks. When I don't think the same way, I get very mixed up."

You sometimes get blamed by your nonalcoholic parent for

problems that the alcoholic parent caused. Maybe that parent has taken money to buy alcohol and then denies it. The next thing you know, you are grounded.

You *know* that you can be confused about which parent to listen to if one of them is alcoholic.

If you ask your alcoholic parent if it is okay to go to a friend's house, he or she just says yes. If you ask the nonalcoholic parent, that parent asks you, "Where you are going? What time are you going to be home?"

You know that your nonalcoholic parent is a better parent to you than the alcoholic. In fact, kids often form a bond to their nonalcoholic parents and get really, really close to them because they care enough to say no. Sometimes, though, you get mad at that parent because of the limits placed on you, especially when the alcoholic would let you go anywhere and do anything (as long as it didn't get in the way of his or her drinking).

You *know* that living in an alcoholic family affects your relationship with your brothers and sisters.

Sometimes you and your brothers or sisters are drawn closer together because of the problems that you share. You actually can be forced to be closer to each other because there is not always anyone else who is able to take care of you and love you. Or you might make efforts to become closer just so that you can help your parent to stop drinking.

Other times brothers and sisters get pushed apart. Alcoholic parents often have pets in the family, and this makes it easy for brothers and sisters to get into fights because of the jealousy and bad feelings that build up. Tom said, "In my case I stick up for my dad when he is sober while my sister sticks up for my mom. My sister goes overboard, always putting my dad down, even when he isn't drunk. That makes us argue. She wonders how I could stand to have anything to do with him at all."

You *know* if you live in an alcoholic family that alcoholism will make your nonalcoholic parent do things for the alcoholic that he or she would never have dreamed of doing for anyone.

In a play we made up, Kim, the wife in the play, was trying to protect Dan, the alcoholic in the play, from the police. Dan had just been fired from his job, gotten drunk, had an accident, and wrecked his car. When the police came she lied for him, saying things like, "I don't know where he is. What did he do? Why are you after him? You must be mistaken."

Husbands and wives of alcoholics often overprotect them. They make excuses for the alcoholics when they can't stop drinking. They put up with abuse and harassment, cleaning up messes after them and trying to be friends to them even when they don't want to be.

They try to keep the alcoholic from drinking. When your alcoholic parent brings home liquor, your nonalcoholic parent will try dumping it down the drain or hiding it.

When all that doesn't help—and it never does—they try to sit down with the alcoholic and talk to them, telling them that their relationships are being ruined and that the drinking has to stop. They even threaten to leave (or actually leave), all to try to get the alcoholic to admit to the problem.

You *know* that when you live with alcoholic parents they do things to make you laugh. You never know whether to laugh or cry, though.

Tom said, "One night my dad came home drunk and couldn't get up the stairs. After about ten tries he finally made it. When he got to the top he was very tired and went to lean on the wall to rest. Where he went to lean, there was no wall, just an open closet. He fell in, broke a few tennis racquets, then got up and went into my room, where he fell on the bed.

"It wasn't funny at the time, but the next day when we all thought how stupid he looked falling through what he thought was a wall and thumping around trying to find his way out of the closet, we all started cracking up."

When you live with an alcoholic, you see drunkenness all the time and you get used to it.

To you, it just becomes normal and it stops being funny, because when a parent is drunk you think about what would happen if there was a fire and he or she was not able to get out in time. Or as one girl said, "There are times you wonder if the alcoholic is going to live to see the next day, like when he or she wakes up in the middle of the night choking."

And you *know* that if you laugh at a parent who is drunk:

You could get hit.

You could hurt his or her feelings.

You could give your parent more of a reason to drink.

After a while, an alcoholic parent's getting drunk makes you so frustrated that you just want to get away from it. You don't want to hear about it; you don't want to see it; you just want to explode! Those are the times that you run to your room and turn on your stereo full-blast because you are so mad.

You *know* that if you live in an alcoholic family it is hard to say what you feel.

You want to get things off your chest, to get rid of the stress that is inside of you because you know it can make you sick. More often than not though, you hide the fact that you have an alcoholic parent.

You hide it because you think that your friends would turn away from you if they knew, and you really don't want to be teased by other kids. You hide it because you are really just trying to make your life easier to bear.

Some kids who live in alcoholic families try to build ideal worlds for their friends to see. They try to do very well in school, to keep up with the latest styles, they try anything to keep the truth away from themselves and people around them. They can even get others believing in their worlds.

They do this in different ways, by:

Keeping their friends away from their parents and lying about what they are like

Making excuses for the alcoholic's drinking

Always avoiding the topic of alcoholism in conversations

Kids try hard to pretend to themselves, too, that one of their parents is not alcoholic. They lie to themselves and say things like, "This isn't really happening to me," and "Oh, my parent doesn't drink much."

They go to school and ignore their home life until they get home. Then they go into their bedrooms and turn up their stereos, put on their headphones and turn on their television sets, or pick up their phones.

Their rooms become their hideaways. They become special places to get away from everything and where they can do everything they want. Dan said, "I know a kid who is eight or nine who has a parent who is alcoholic. He sometimes gets into a fantasy world, and it is hard for him to break away from it. He actually gives an imaginary friend a personality, and if he has a problem with his parent he goes into his imaginary world."

They pretend by blocking all their feelings and trying to make themselves feel happy by thinking happy thoughts.

Paul M. said, "I used to fantasize a lot, I used to imagine being the greatest pianist, the greatest pilot. I was kind of a loner and would detach myself, spend a lot of time by myself. I would make my own dreams."

You *know* that if one of your parents is alcoholic, it doesn't mean that you don't love him or her any longer. You do get angry more often; you do feel hate and fury. You feel those things though, because you do love your parent and you don't want that parent killing himself or herself.

Finally, you *know* that you can survive living with an alcoholic parent, because you do have some choices (like talking about it), but you *know* that it is very hard. You *know* there are a lot of things to survive:

Not enough attention
Too many responsibilities
Drunken abuse
Looking for your parent

Fear of divorce
Embarrassment
Shame
A lack of friends

Not Enough Attention

"When I was drinking real heavy, my kids weren't with me, they were with my daughter. I would have rather gone out drinking than travel two and a half hours to see them. Looking back, it makes me kind of ashamed of myself really."—Judy S., recovering alcoholic.

You need love from your parents. If one of your parents is alcoholic, it makes it harder for either of them to give you the love you need.

Your nonalcoholic parent might pay more attention to you to try to make up for the attention that the alcoholic parent doesn't give you. But often that parent can't keep up, even though he or she is trying hard all the time. Face it, he or she is just too busy taking care of your alcoholic parent.

It is easy for you to suffer because of this, and you can get yourself into all sorts of trouble just trying to get some of the attention you need.

Many kids from alcoholic families drink to try to get attention, some with their alcoholic parents, others behind their parents' backs, as Meg said, "to drown their own sorrows."

Where kids can really have problems is in school. Their grades can get very low if their parents are alcoholic because it can make them fail to care. They are always so preoccupied with their parents that they can't pay attention or even think straight.

Jim P., whose stepfather is alcoholic, said, "Life at home with an alcoholic parent can bring you pretty much into the gutter. They try to run your life when they can't even run their own. 'Do this, do that.' My stepfather has been saying to me, 'You're stupid, you can't do nothing.' He makes me feel bad.

"It isn't easy to separate your life at home from your life at school. I have had thirty-two days of in-school suspension this year. About twenty-nine of them are a result of home. It is like, people at home, they tell you what to do and you have to follow it. So I take it out on people at school because I can get away with it."

Too Many Responsibilities

"When I was younger, I never got to do anything. I never got to be a kid because I had so much responsibility."—Keith Thompson, age fourteen.

The first thing we would say to a kid who doesn't have too much responsibility because of alcoholism in a parent is, "You are lucky!" At the same time as you are having to learn to take care of yourself and be more independent, you are having to grow up as well. You just have to put more time into your family, because the alcoholic parent really doesn't care about anything except the booze.

You have to do things like go off to school and then come home right afterward to clean the house. Or you have to stay home after school to take care of younger brothers and sisters. This is really boring and makes you feel like you don't have any freedom at all.

You think, "This is a drag. I've done too much, too quickly, and I should be able to do things a kid does and not be tied down. If I even wanted to do something on my own, my brother or sister would want to do something totally different."

All of the responsibilities make you feel embarrassed and uncomfortable around your friends. You get filled with anger and worry about things like, "I hope when I come home with my friends my mom doesn't have the house a mess, with liquor bottles all over the floor. If that's the way it is, then I won't ever be able to forgive her." Or "If I brought my friend over, could I trust him [or her] not to go back to the kids in school and say what my family is really like?"

All of this keeps you tired and in a bad mood a lot of the time, feeling left out of the other things kids do, like:

Getting into sports
Having time by themselves
Just playing after school
Having good friends

After a while, you just start to assume that you have to do everything yourself. Instead of your parents taking care of you, you are taking care of your parents. For this, you can feel hate and anger; you lose respect for the alcoholic because he or she can't be in control.

Drunken Abuse

When you get hit by a drunken parent, it is painful—physically and mentally. If you got up on a Saturday morning and someone grabbed you by the hair, picked you up, and hit you against a wall a couple of times, you would know the feeling.

Violence from alcoholic parents is mostly caused by their lack of knowing what they are doing when they are drunk. Some don't even know when they are abusing their kids. They are just bombed out of their minds and they do whatever their alcohol affected minds tell them to do. (That is why, too, there is a great connection between alcoholism and sexual abuse of kids. Alcohol makes people do things they normally wouldn't dream of doing.)

Many parents who hit you will stop if you start crying, but alcoholic parents will be more likely to say something like, "Now I will really give you something to cry about." Then they will hit you again and again.

Judy S. said, "My kids saw me drunk quite a few times. I would be kind of funny and stumble, and they would laugh at me. Sometimes it made me very mad at them. I would say something like, 'Don't you all laugh at me!' They would say, 'You're so funny, we can't help it.' Then I would chase after them saying, 'I'm going to beat you up!'

"But I never really did beat them up that I know of. There was one time, though, with my one older daughter, when she began laughing at me and told me I was drunk. I said, 'No I'm not and don't you laugh at me!' I went after her and knocked her down."

From our experiences, alcoholic fathers become more violent than alcoholic mothers. If your mother is alcoholic, the house is more likely to be a mess; she won't care where you went or what time you are coming home. With an alcoholic mother there may be more yelling and screaming.

With alcoholic fathers, there seems to be more hitting. They go off like bullet shots. When they go off, you can get hit for the littlest things, like:

Spilling your milk on the floor

Wearing something they don't like

Getting a B on a test

Talking back

Hitting your brother

Once it's over, they are likely to forget all about it. You don't. Perhaps that is why kids in alcoholic families have a lot of nightmares. They can be so scared of alcoholic parents beating the tar out of them that they wake up in a cold sweat, having dreamed that it happened.

Dreams like that can make you wish that the alcoholic in your life was dead. You can wish that your alcoholic mother or father would just trip down the stairs and hit their heads (a drunken parent will fall down the stairs a lot, anyway). This can be an upsetting thing to think, because even if your parents are alcoholic and beat you, you can care very much for them. It is easy, though, to have get-even thoughts.

Sometimes you may even feel like killing your parent. Keith said, "I imagined putting knives up through my stepfather's bed when he was sleeping or drilling holes through his forehead. I didn't do these things, but I felt like I could have."

Having these feelings can make you feel good sometimes and evil and wicked other times. Nate said, "I have been reading this book called, *To Be a Killer*. The kid in the book is under a lot of pressure. He was great in school and great in football, but he finally becomes a killer because everybody is on his back. It is sort of the same thing in an alcoholic family; you feel like everybody is always on your back."

Of course, we don't think that you should kill anybody, but these are common thoughts for kids who are trying to survive living with an alcoholic parent.

Looking for Your Parent

Alcoholics are often late in coming home. This is scary because you don't know where they are, what the problems are, or why they are so late, and you think that maybe they will never come home again. You think, too, that anything that happens to them is your fault because you didn't know how to stop them from going out in the first place. When you think that, it is horrible.

It is true that sometimes you wish your alcoholic parent wouldn't come home at all, because you know that once he or she comes home, something is going to happen. Usually, you worry right up until your parent comes home, and then you are relieved but very, very angry.

Many times you get so worried while waiting that you and your family go looking for the alcoholic parent. This is hard, because your parent can be anywhere.

Keith told us about a time that his stepfather disappeared. "My mom had just married my stepfather. On one Friday, actually his birthday, he decided that he wanted to go play pool with a friend. So he stopped by the house and gave his check to my mother and told her that he would be gone for a few hours.

"She waited and waited for him to come back. Finally, my stepfather's friend's wife called looking for her husband. My mom said that she hadn't seen either him or my stepfather. So my mom went out looking all over town for the two of them and never did find them. He showed up three days later. I was in the first grade then and we were living in Connecticut. My stepfather had gone to Maine for the weekend without telling us."

If you go looking for and find alcoholic parents, it is important not to be mean or nasty. You have to take it very easy with them and talk to them a lot, without yelling or mentioning anything about where they were or what they did. You can't argue. You have to get them sober, then discuss the problems with them.

You may find that after you go looking for alcoholic parents a few times, it starts to feel like a waste of time. Wherever you do find them (usually at some unknown friend's house or bar) they don't know what they are doing.

This can be totally embarrassing and can tick you off pretty badly, because you have to try somehow to persuade them to go home and go to bed. At this point they will get mad at you for looking at all and will even attack you. It seems to make them think that you don't think they can take care of themselves. (They actually can't.)

Fear of Divorce

Alcoholism causes parents to fight.

Paul M., a recovering alcoholic who grew up in an alcoholic family, said, "My parents used to fight and argue all the time. I was caught in between the two of them. My mother thought I was the Messiah, the Lord God Almighty, and my father thought I was a dunce.

"So they would battle over me. My mother would get drunk and I could hear them arguing out there. My father would be saying, 'Well, he is never going to amount to anything.' Then my mother would come into my room crying and she would shake me and say, 'Son, tell me you are going to amount to something.' I would say, 'Mom, I just want to get some sleep. Amount to something? I'm only twelve years old.' "

When parents fight, kids get afraid of a divorce. When one of your parents is alcoholic, you are *always* afraid of divorce. The truth is, they seem to go together.

Kids always think that parents should be able to work out problems and stay together. If your mother or father is drunk every night, your other parent can get very bored and very mad.

Let's say one of your parents, your father, drinks all the time and uses all the family money for alcohol. He can appear to your mother to be married to the bottle and not to her! This could make her so mad that she will finally say, "This has got to stop. I can't stay up nights waiting to see if you are going to be drunk or not. I have to go on with my life."

Divorces don't make the alcoholism better. Some may make it worse. However, a sober parent may want a divorce just to get away from the problems caused by the alcoholism. Problems like:

Mental and physical abuse
Constant embarrassment
Repeated lying
Hurt feelings
Ruined lives

How long your sober parent will wait before divorcing depends on what kind of drunk the alcoholic is. For example, if he is violent, your mother wouldn't be likely to stay as long as if your alcoholic father is a quiet drunk.

Kids have different opinions about how long parents should work on the problem before splitting up. Some say, "However long it takes, until the alcoholic is able to say that he or she has a problem." Others say, "Stay together as long as the alcoholic cares enough and is willing to try. But if the alcoholic has a bad attitude, maybe you should give up."

We interviewed Keith's mother about her life with Keith's stepfather and her decision to divorce. She told us:

"Living with my ex-husband was like being in a play. Everybody had a part and everybody was expected to play his or her part. After a while you just got used to playing the part and you didn't want to change it because you had learned how to deal with it and how to cope with it.

"My ex-husband was drinking from the time I first met him. I was brought up in a very restricted background— there was no drinking in our family—and I really didn't know what an alcoholic was.

"I think because of that I denied a lot in those first four years. To myself, I just said, 'He's just a big drinker. He drinks a lot, and I don't. How can I say that he's wrong, because I don't know anything about this?' I denied the problem until it got to the point where I couldn't ignore it anymore. Like when he would go to the store for a pack of cigarettes and come back four hours later. He would disappear for three days. He would take the car and knock down guardrails when he was drunk. Things like that caused me to recognize there was a problem.

"By that time, we were so far into our parts that it was real difficult to break that barrier and he had a real hold on the family. There was no democracy in our family; it was a total dictatorship.

"Life was unpredictable. You would come in the evening and you didn't know what you were going to find, a friendly or an abusive person. The kids and I developed signals. I would give a signal that it was okay to be laughing. Another signal would mean, You better go to your room. It was one of those times.

"He treated the boys extremely cruelly. I'll give you an example: When Keith's brother, Kyle, was younger, he did something at the table which his stepfather didn't like very much, so he grabbed Kyle by the back of his neck and dragged him up the stairs with a bowl of water and told him that if he was going to act like an animal at the table, we are going to treat him like one. Kyle was made to stay like that the whole evening. He also made Keith stay in his room for six weeks. He wasn't allowed to eat with the family, he wasn't allowed to speak with the family.

"Violence prevailed with the kids, and he was verbally cruel to me. He would say things to me which were so bad that my opinion of myself became very low. I tried everything that I could while we were married to make it work. I went to Al-Anon and alcohol education classes for a year and a half. I kept hoping that I could find a way to live with the situation, because I really was in love with this man. Even two years after the divorce, I was still wanting to get back together. I would have done anything that I could. There was just no way.

"I guess there was about four years that we lived together, where all I had going for me was counseling sessions just to hold on. I got to the point where I couldn't do that anymore. I didn't have the strength or the desire.

"When we finally divorced, there was relief. Loads of responsibility were lifted off everyone's shoulders. It is a big responsibility living with an alcoholic father and an alcoholic husband.

"What I realize now is that if you live with an alcoholic, you are not helping yourself, your family, or him by making it easy for him. I think that if I had confronted him early on with how I felt, there was a chance that it might have stopped him. But I didn't, I helped him.

"I have done a lot of things now, after the divorce, that I wanted to do all my life. I am not dependent on anyone emotionally. I have learned that I can be a person, an individual, and have a lot of things that I can do. I have gone back to school. I am growing, and after years of having that stifled, I don't want anything to change that. I have worked too hard for it."

Parents don't automatically get divorced because of alcoholism. Most couples try to work out their problems. The truth is though that alcoholism changes people's feelings about each other and can ruin a relationship between a husband and a wife very easily.

Embarrassment

All children who live in alcoholic families react differently to situations they face.

You may have feelings of hate when your parent beats you, then gets sober and asks you how you got the bruises. When your parent is drunk you may feel hurt, depressed, and scared because you don't understand what is going on.

One of the most common feelings for kids who grow up in alcoholic families is embarrassment. You get embarrassed when your parent comes home and passes out on the floor, or anywhere in the house for that matter, while a friend of yours is there. You get embarrassed when a friend is over at your house and your parent tries to pressure him or her into drinking.

And there are other things that embarrass you:

When you bring a friend home and you find a big party going on.

When your class is going on a field trip. Your dad is invited to come as a chaperon and he shows up drunk.

When your whole family goes to a restaurant and your drunk parent gets violent.

Even though embarrassment is one of the most common feelings, it is not the most difficult emotion kids who live in alcoholic families have to handle. It is actually much easier to handle the embarrassment than it is to handle the shame.

Shame

You know that you are ashamed of your parent when you find yourself trying to:

Get good grades
Do a lot of reading
Work hard to get yourself on the honor roll all just to cover it up.

Alcoholic parents can get bad reputations, not only for themselves but also for their kids; this is a real pressure for the kids. It causes you to worry about getting picked on and to worry that other parents may not let their kids hang around you because it is too dangerous.

Michelle, a thirteen-year-old girl, said, "Whenever my grandfather got drunk and the police came to get him, my mother and uncles would be too ashamed to go to school because it was as if everyone had found out."

You are ashamed when your parent loses a job and you begin to think that your parent is incapable of even keeping one. You are ashamed about money and think, "Boy, I hope my mom [or dad] finds another job soon. I'm in junior high and I have to have good clothes or I'll be called a grub."

It seems as if you are always feeling ashamed because of things your parent might do. You worry that your mother or father might be in jail because of driving drunk or fighting; or you worry that your parent has been injured in an accident while drinking and driving or, even worse, that your parent has killed somebody.

The shame you feel causes you to not want to be seen around the alcoholic. Joanie Turner, a thirteen-year-old girl, said, "My parents don't allow my alcoholic family members to come into our house with beer because they don't want other kids to make fun of us. My mom tells me not to pay attention, but it is hard and I don't think that I can go through that again and again."

It can get so bad that sometimes you and your family will plot against the alcoholic. It can become like a complex military plan: You talk behind the alcoholic's back, you go out and eat without him or her, all just to avoid the shame of being seen together in public. This makes you feel bad. What is worse, you become ashamed that you are ashamed.

A Lack of Friends

One of the hardest things about growing up in a family where one of your parents (or grandparents for that matter) is alcoholic is what it does to your friendships.

Since you don't want to go around announcing to the world that someone in your family drinks too much, and since no one else who lives in a family where someone abuses alcohol says much about it either, you usually end up believing that you are completely alone. What this does is make you feel different from every other kid you see. To you, different means "not as good" at best.

Almost always you walk around in school or around your community feeling jealous of kids you see who look like they have the "perfect families" that you have always dreamed of having. You know . . . families where mothers and fathers talk over things together without constant fighting, crying, or arguments, families where everyone eats together rather than where, like yours, mother is in the bedroom drunk and asleep or dad is at the bar drinking the evening away.

Living with an alcoholic parent just makes you feel afraid of other kids. It is as simple as that. You might know enough to realize that your parent gets drunk all of the time because he or she has a "problem" or a disease and that you don't. The truth, though, is that you automatically assume something is wrong with *you*, and if there wasn't, you would be like the kids you see who seem to live in those perfect families.

Since you think something is wrong with you, really wrong, you figure that you don't deserve the attention and the self-confidence that other kids seem to have. After all, hasn't your mother told you what a rotten kid you are? Or hasn't your dad said that you were stupid, not worth a dime? Sure they were drunk when they said these things, but what does that have to do with it?

So you stay back from other kids. You don't give them a chance to get to know you. If you did, you are certain they would eventually see through you. They would see after a while that you are truly the rotten, stupid kid your parents already know you are anyway. When this happens, and you know it always will, they won't want to be friends of yours anyway. In your mind it is much easier to push them away first, rather than take a chance in being hurt.

Kids from alcoholic families don't always know that they are doing this when they do it. We think many times they do though. You always carry around with you a little voice that reminds you to "stay back." It is like a warning signal that goes off whenever it looks like you are going to get too close to anyone.

There are a number of ways that kids keep themselves from making friends. Some of them can be pretty tricky really.

What we mean is that to someone else, a kid from an alcoholic family can sometimes look like he or she is getting real close to a friend. What only the kid knows, though, is that he or she is really not there at all.

Here are some examples of what we mean.

One way that you keep from having real friends is to be a total loner. You go to school, but you are real quiet. You sit by yourself in classes. You eat by yourself in lunch. Teachers worry about you. They ask you how you are doing occasionally. Basically, they leave you alone though because you tell them, "Great" or "Fine," and don't give them a chance to ask any more questions. You do the same with any kids who want to try to be your friends, too.

If someone asks you over to his or her house after school or to a dance on Friday night, you make excuses. You have to baby-sit. You are going away for the weekend. Sometimes you pretend not to hear the question. Most of the time, you don't ever get the question asked because you have done such a good job at giving everyone signals that you want to be by yourself.

Another way that you might keep friends away is to be perfect. This way is confusing to people around you (and for that matter to your self) because you look like you are completely with it, in the swing of things. In fact, you are completely out of them all the time.

Nonetheless, you dress perfectly. You get perfect grades. You talk perfectly. You hang around with the other perfect kids in school (ones whose families look like the perfect family to you—you know, with parents who live together, who have money and drive fancy cars). Mostly, you spend time with them at *their* houses, though, never at yours. This way you can make up stories about your family that makes them look wonderful. You don't have to answer questions about why your house is a mess, why your parents fight, why your father was arrested. Or why he hit you the night before.

To the kids you hang out with, it looks like you're totally perfect. The best of friends. You know you aren't, though. Inside, you know how hard you have to work at looking good, at keeping up what you think is the image that they like. No matter how well, how perfectly you do anything, you never think you do enough. After a while, you start to run out of energy for this. Your head hurts. Or you get stomachaches. And you know that eventually your friends are going to find out that the perfect kid they see isn't real. Naturally, they won't like you then. So you move on to some other group of "perfect" friends before this happens.

There is one more, very common way that kids from alcoholic families stay isolated from other kids. They become "rebels." When you decide to do this, it is because your life has been so much different than everyone (in your mind) else's for so long that you end up saying to yourself, "What's the point of being just like everyone else anyway? I never have and I never will, so I might as well be an 'individual.' I will do whatever I want to. Right?"

When you live in a family with an alcoholic, you do get pretty used to being different, to living differently. That is true. You see the world in ways that most kids your age never do. You see yourself as being older and younger all at once. You know how to handle incredible things like calling the ambulance when your father passes out on the floor and goes into convulsions. (Of course, when he is sober, you are not allowed to cross the street.)

You do get pretty tired of trying to be like "one of them," other kids who don't live with the pressures and frustrations that you live with. This way of acting, of being a rebel, usually gets you more attention than being a loner. This feels good sometimes. It also gets you kids to hang out with. Other rebels. In the end, though, it's no different than being alone because the other kids you choose as friends, the rebels, don't know a whole lot about being good friends anyway. And believe it or not, when you grow up in an alcoholic family, you can always imagine even the biggest loser in the world finding out that you are nothing more than a bad unit and rejecting you.

You Do Have Some Choices

The hardest thing about living with an alcoholic parent is deciding what to do about it. Luckily, you do have some choices.

Never Argue with a Drunk: Leave drunken parents alone, ignore them. Keith said, "On Saturday morning or when we would have days off, I would always know my stepfather was up when he would cough, so on those days I tried to say in bed as long as I could. I tried to avoid him as much as possible."

Drunk: Never argue with me.

Interviewer: Why not?

Drunk: You never win. You can't prove I'm wrong.

Interviewer: Why can't I prove you wrong if you *are* wrong?

Drunk: Because I'm always right. If I'm always right, then I'm always right.

When parents are drunk, they don't know what they are doing and they get upset easily. Also, they will stick to their sides of stories no matter what facts you have, because they really and truly think that they are right. Keith said, "I remember when I would come home and see my stepfather hitting the bottle hard. When he tried to tell me something I knew was wrong, I tried to tell him that it was not true. This made me feel so angry and helpless. It was a losing battle."

If your parent is drunk, going to your room and being alone is a good thing to do, especially when you feel like you are going to punch your mother or your alcoholic father. This a good time to find a pillow and beat it.

If your parent is drunk, call someone to talk to or just avoid being in the house so that you don't get beaten or injured if the parent does something crazy—like throwing things around the house.

Go to a relative's house
Go to a friend's house
Ride your bicycle
Take a walk

Go for Outside Help: Another choice you have is to go for outside help rather than think you can handle the problem of alcoholism alone.

One boy said, "I know a thirteen-year-old boy who came home and found his parents drunk. They started beating him up with a belt and with a stick, so he took off and went to a friend's house who lived a couple miles away. He asked his friend's parents if he could stay over because he was being beaten. They said yes and then called the police and told them what had happened."

A lot of kids from alcoholic homes run away. Keith said, "I considered it." One girl said, "I ran away. I felt scared that he would find me." Another girl said, "I tried it one time and didn't get away with it. I got halfway down the road, looked back, and there was his car."

In kids' minds there are good reasons to leave, especially if one of your parents is violent and your other parent doesn't do anything about the problem. Kids think when this happens that they have to do something to protect themselves and get help. They go places where they have someone who will allow them to stay for a while, like an older sister's or brother's house or, if their parents are divorced, the nonalcoholic parent's house.

The important thing is to know what you are doing before you leave. You could get yourself into much more trouble than you are already in.

You can decide, too, not to try all by yourself to make your parent stop drinking. There are alcohol specialists you can go to for help. When your parent is sober, you probably think you should try to help by trying to talk your parent out of drinking again. But what usually happens is that alcoholic parents want you to leave them alone.

Really, someone else's drinking is hard to stop. We asked Paul M., a recovering alcoholic, if he thought his kids could have ever convinced him to stop drinking. He said, "I don't think so. I am kind of a soft-hearted individual basically, and I think if they came to me and said, with tears in their eyes, 'Please, Daddy, stop drinking,' I might have said, 'Well, I will go on the wagon,' but I think I would have been drinking somewhere down the road. I don't think anybody can stop you but yourself. It takes realizing that you have a problem, then doing something about it."

If you spend all your energy trying to get a parent not to drink, it really sidetracks you. It interrupts your schoolwork and your friendships, because you only have time for whoever you are trying to help. And it almost never works.

Make the Best of a Divorce: Parents protect their alcoholic husbands or wives because they love them very much, so much so that they don't want to see them go. Love doesn't fade away just because of problems. That love can go away, though, if things don't get better.

If your parents do separate and divorce, you will be nervous and feel really bad inside. You will feel like you want to be with both parents equally, and you won't be able to understand why you can't.

You won't know how to handle the feelings. You may be afraid that you will never see one of your parents again or that after a divorce you won't be able to spend enough time with either of your parents. You will worry about getting caught in the middle. You will think, "Oh, if my parents get divorced, which one do I want to live with?"

The best thing to try to do if this happens is to stay calm. Stop and think about the whole situation and try to forgive whoever you are mad at. Remember, too, that it is not *your* fault. After the divorce you may really feel better than you did before, because you might not have so much trouble from the alcoholic parent.

Sometimes you wish your parents *would* get divorced. You wish that because you have dreams that if the alcoholic parent left you might be able to have normal friendships or a normal family. Every kid has his or her own idea of a perfect family: maybe a father and a mother, living in a big house, on a hill, in the country with two cars, a dog, and a cat.

Of course, everyone's fantasy is a little different and there is no normal, really. But every kid who lives in an alcoholic family dreams about, at least, not having an alcoholic parent.

We suggest that if you have this wish, try to talk to someone about it. This wish could hurt the feelings of your alcoholic and your nonalcoholic parent. Kim Peterson, one of the authors, said, "I would say, 'Wait a minute, your parents may love you. You just have to help them out. Help them get over the alcoholism. If you help them out, I would imagine that you would love your parents as much as they really love you.' "

But this is a normal wish for kids who live in alcoholic families, so if you have it, don't feel bad.

Talk About It: If you live in an alcoholic family, you are usually afraid to talk about:

Arguments in the family
Fights in the family
Getting beaten
Someone being drunk

Because of the shame and embarrassment of these situations, you don't want it all over town. You're not really sure what family life is supposed to be like, and since everyone wants their family to be normal, you get afraid that people will laugh at you or make fun of you if they find out yours is not.

You're just plain afraid. You're afraid to say anything to anyone because maybe you're afraid of it getting back to the alcoholic. Say you tell something to your friend and your friend tells his friend, who tells his mother, and the mother knows your father and talks to him. You don't want it to get back to him because maybe he'll do something rash, like yell at you or hit you. Maybe you'll go home to a blackout and a beating.

The problem is that if you don't talk about your life in an alcoholic family, you become very unhappy. You can even explode if it just stays bottled up inside you and builds up. You will walk around wondering:

Why me?
Can I help my family?
What kind of mood will my dad/mom be in when I get home?
When am I going to get beaten next?
Are my parents going to be fighting tonight?

And you will stay tied up with feelings of:

Anger
Disgust
Despair
Helplessness
Frustration
Sadness

You will stay caught between love and hate, always in pain, always thinking that you are useless and no good and that everything is all your fault.

Some kids try to deal with the feelings themselves. If you do, it can make you sick or can cause you to behave badly. You might start arguments with anyone who says anything to you, or you may blame everything bad that happens to you on others. You might start saying things that aren't true and then seeing yourself as a liar or a messed-up person.

Worst of all, you might just break down from holding in your feelings and start to withdraw from everyone around you. You might even think about killing yourself.

This is a common feeling if you are the son or the daughter of an alcoholic. You think you are the only one with problems. When that happens, you start to think that you don't mean anything to anyone. The more you try to hide it, the more it just keeps you all mixed up, growing worse every day you hold it in. It makes you feel like an empty room, like you're dead already.

If this happens to you, you have to realize you need help. You need to talk it out for the sake of your life. Find a friend you trust and say, "Hey, my family and I have a big mess up at our house. Could you help?" Try to talk about what's wrong.

Some kids might say that you can only trust people you have known for a while. You don't always have to know a person for a long time to know if he or she can be trusted, though.

Other kids will say it's easier to trust a relative. This can be true, but you may just want somebody to talk to who doesn't know you, because sometimes the closer you are to a person, the more embarrassed you're going to be when you bring a problem up. (Also, if it is a grandparent or another relative who is alcoholic, too, he or she will not want to believe there is a problem!)

There are ways to begin to trust by testing a person out. When you want to trust someone, the person's attitude will be very important to you. If you have a friend who ignores you a lot, this is not a good sign. If someone says that he or she is a friend of yours but then talks about you behind your back, this is also a problem.

The first thing to do is to pay attention to a person's viewpoints on other matters. Who is he or she friends with? What are his or her parents like? For example, Nate has a friend who hangs around him and does stupid things all the time, like throwing bottles at signs. Nate thinks he is okay to play with, but he would never talk to him about anything personal. If he did, Nate would be afraid that his friend would think it was funny and then laugh and clown around. Maybe he would even use it against Nate sometime.

Next, you could ask the person to discuss a problem, not the one that you really want to talk about, but another one. Maybe you could tell your friend something that is not so important to you and see if that person would tell another person. If you hear it around the school, then you will know that your friend has told someone else.

Finally, if the person you are talking to has already told you something important, if that person trusts you, you probably can trust him or her. You might not want to say, "You should tell me something so that I can see if I can trust you or not." If one day the person just comes up and tells you something that is really awful, really important, then you can feel pretty sure that you can trust them.

You might go to an Al-Anon meeting, although this can be hard for a kid. If you can't talk once you get there, don't run out. Just say, "I can't go through with it now," and listen to what others have to say. Or you might try finding someone with the same problem and go to Al-Anon with them.

If you are a kid in an alcoholic family, it is important to try to begin to believe that someone you can trust cares about you and will understand you. When you finally do talk about it with someone, it helps you and makes you feel a whole lot better.

The first time you do, it is like a burst of all the bad feelings coming out of you at once. It is great! It is like getting rid of something painful, the shame and the embarrassment that you have carried around for a long time.

You Can Trust: Trust is believing in somebody else. Trust is believing that a person will not do anything to hurt you. Trusting others gives you a good foundation in your life; you need to trust to feel okay about yourself.

Growing up in an alcoholic family causes you to take a long time to trust anyone. You have a barrier inside. You try to get through the barrier but you can't. It just doesn't work.

This barrier makes trusting very difficult, because in order to trust someone you really have to get to know a person. You have to talk to that person a lot. This can be scary if you are not used to it. You can do it, though.

What we are saying is not to be too afraid to find out if you can trust others. Some things won't be easy to share (like if your parent or relative did something terrible), but overall it is good to talk about any problem dealing with alcoholism.

You will get hurt sometimes. Everybody does. But, if you really need to talk, and you know you can trust someone, it will make your life easier. If you don't take the chance, you may miss one of the best experiences you may ever have.

Face the Truth: The most important choice that kids in alcoholic families can make is to accept that a parent is an alcoholic rather than pretending the problem doesn't exist.

No matter how hard you try to deny it, you will always know the truth. It will get out in the open one way or another. Once you do accept it and talk about it, you can begin to believe that the drinking is not your problem, that it is the problem of the drinker and nothing you can control.

A Test

Kids can have parents who are alcoholic and actually never realize that it is a problem. Keith said, "Until I was about ten years old, I thought that everybody was alcoholic. I thought that everybody was intensely drunk all the time. I didn't realize they weren't until I spent a couple weeks with my grandmother." One girl said, "When I was about five years old, my father drank a lot and his friend did the same, so I thought that everybody did." Another girl said, "As a little girl, I thought that all fathers were drunk and all mothers weren't."

If you are a child who lives in an alcoholic family and you don't spend much time out of your house with your friends, you won't understand that everybody doesn't live the same way you do.

Here is a test to help you know if something is wrong.

Test:
Is Your Parent an Alcoholic?

Does your parent ever come home in a rage?

Does your parent ever beat you?

Does your parent get drunk every time he or she drinks?

Does your parent have a drink after work pretty routinely?

Does your parent sometimes smell like alcohol when talking?

Does your parent's personality change after having a drink or two?

Does your parent keep a lot of alcohol in the house?

Does your parent have bottles of alcohol along all the time (on trips, at parties)?

Does your parent always have bloodshot eyes the day after?

Does your parent sometimes sneak alcohol?

Does your parent occasionally smash things and break them after drinking?

Does your parent always go to the refrigerator a lot, say, during television commercials?

Have the police ever come to your house?

Does your parent wreck a lot of cars each year?

Has your parent ever been arrested while drinking?

Does your parent get sick a lot or miss days of work?

If you answer yes to any five of these, your parent likely has a problem with alcohol. If that is the case, we think that you should begin thinking about talking to someone: your counselor, your minister, your doctor.

It could be worth it, because alcoholic parents can get better. Plenty have.

Chapter VI

Getting Better

When you live in an alcoholic family, you sometimes lie in bed at night and dream. You dream that your parents are going to quit drinking, that you are going to get closer to them. You are going to have a better life.

You picture your parents beginning to care for themselves and for you. You imagine it being beautiful. Your house is clean and organized. Instead of abusing you, or being nice to you just to get rid of you, your parents are helping you with your homework. They are starting to think things out. Instead of just saying yes or no right away when you ask them questions, they are saying, "We'll think about it."

Anyone Can Do It

All alcoholic parents don't recover, and if they don't recover, they die from alcoholism one way or another. They damage their livers, have heart attacks, or get into car and other accidents.

If your parents don't recover, you *have* to be realistic. You can't go through life in a constant dream, because if your dream keeps growing and growing and nothing changes, you will always live in a fantasy world. One day you will just simply give up.

If you find yourself in an alcoholic family where cousins, aunts, uncles, grandparents, or parents are alcoholic, though, you don't have to just dream. They *can* recover. They can recover if they understand why they drink and if they begin to get involved with life around them—without alcohol.

And you know what? Anyone can do it.

It Isn't Exactly Easy

We aren't saying that it is easy for alcoholics to recover. The road to recovery is hard, and there are plenty of things that can get in the way.

If your alcoholic parents quit drinking, they will probably lose their drinking friends. If they are the only friends they have (which is most likely the case after years of alcoholic drinking), it will make it hard for your parents to stop.

Some of your relatives may even put pressure on your parents to keep drinking. Kelly Bradshaw, a thirteen-year-old girl we interviewed, said, "My mother wanted my stepfather to keep drinking because he was always a grump when he didn't drink." Some relatives who drink will want your parents to keep drinking because they might spoil all the "fun" in the family by quitting. They also wouldn't know how to react to them sober.

Then there are people who are not alcoholic who don't really know how hard it is to quit. While your parents are trying to stop they encourage them to drink. Their problem is that they don't know how to act around your parents if they weren't drinking.

It Takes More Than
a Lot of Willpower

It takes more than a lot of willpower to be successful in recovering from alcoholism. Willpower is when you walk into your kitchen and, while on a diet, drool over a big batch of brownies—without eating one!

For your alcoholic parents to give up alcohol is not quite as simple as just not eating brownies when they want some. For them to give up alcohol is quite painful. Liken it to the sting of a needle.

Pretend that you were going to give up food for an entire year of your life. It would be pretty hard. You would feel very empty. We have never gone through it, but we bet that each alcoholic who does give up alcohol has a feeling of this kind.

We asked Mr. David O'Brien, an alcohol treatment specialist, what he thought the hardest part of giving up alcohol would be for people who are alcoholic. He said, "When alcoholics begin to recover, the first problem that they have to face is learning to live without this 'friend' called alcohol.

"They really do lose a friend. A friend they have relied on, escaped to, and been counseled by. In the early part of treatment that loss is the hardest of things for them to accept.

"In fact, the acceptance of that loss is the lesson most treatment programs try to examine. In Alcoholics Anonymous, for example, the first thing alcoholics are made aware of is how to separate themselves from alcohol. Even though they may have marriage, job, legal, and money problems, they first start working on the alcohol problem. If they work on that, the other problems can come around, but if they worry about the other problems first, they'll never lick the alcohol problem."

There Are Some Ways You Cannot Help

If you live in an alcoholic family, you're always looking for a way to help your parents to recover. You can go for a while ignoring them and taking care of yourself, but you always end up trying to help, even though it is not the best thing for you to do.

There are some ways you can help your parents in their recoveries from alcoholism, but there are other ways you cannot. These are some common ways children try that cannot help.

Running Away: Say you decide you are going to try to get your parent to go for help. You say to yourself, "I want to make my dad [or mom] think twice and remember that there is a kid in this house—me—who needs to be cared for." So you decide to run away from home to try to get their attention.

What you probably think is that your parent is going to get very upset, quit drinking, and go to Alcoholics Anonymous because he or she is afraid of losing you. That usually isn't what happens.

As we said before, running away from home is not *always* a bad idea. If your parent is abusing you, running away is good as long as you have the chance go to live in a (good) foster home, a friend's house, an aunt's, uncle's, or divorced parent's house (who isn't alcoholic, of course).

Frank Stephenson is a thirteen-year-old boy who ran away from home because of his alcoholic stepfather. Frank said, "He was always drinking and slapping us around, not just me but my brothers, too. One day I left early in the morning and I didn't tell him why. When I came home from school later that day, my stepfather said that he was going to tell my mother all about me leaving early without permission. Then he grounded me. Whenever he grounded me he would hit me, and I decided right then that I wasn't going to take it anymore.

"I didn't really want to run away. I had thought many times about leaving, but I hadn't because I was worried about my younger brothers. But that day I went to my father's house. He wasn't home when I got there, but I waited around. When he got home he said, 'What are you doing here?' He asked me if I was here to stay the night or to live. I said, 'To live.' And he said, 'We'll see what your mother says.'

"When we went back to my mother's house she at first said no. But we talked about it, and after all the talking was done she asked me if I still wanted to live with my father. I told her that I did, and she told me to get out. I did.

"Things are much better now. The only problem is that I can't have my lamp or my teddy bear back. My mother won't give them to me."

Running away can be useful if you know where you are going and why you are going, but running away to get a parent to stop drinking or to get help just doesn't work. It usually only makes matters worse. It will more than likely make your parent mad at you, and you could get beaten or emotionally abused (your parent may call you all kinds of names or say things that might really scare you!). This will make you feel like nobody cares for you anymore and as if the running away was, in the end, all in vain.

Getting Rid of the Alcohol: Another way you might try to help your parents recover from alcoholism is by getting rid of all the alcohol in the house. You might think that dumping out an alcoholic's alcohol or diluting it with water (milk makes it taste awful) might cause your alcoholic parents to stop drinking.

It doesn't. Kelly Bradshaw, the thirteen-year-old girl we interviewed, said, "I once took a vodka bottle and threw it at my father in an attempt to get him to stop drinking. It smashed right in front of him and it did have an effect. The effect was that he went right out and got another bottle. After that I didn't talk to him for two weeks, which made him stop drinking for a while, but not for long."

Thinking About Hurting Yourself: When you get really mad, this is something that you might think will help.

Here is a typical situation: It is evening and you are in your room. In the other room your parents are fighting over the fact that one of them is constantly coming home late—and drunk. You are going crazy with anger, so you turn your stereo up to drown out the bickering.

You keep getting madder and madder, and your mind takes you away into a world where you are all alone. You try to avoid getting this mad, because all it does is fill you with hate and resentment. This time you have gotten too mad.

All of a sudden you don't know what you're doing and you start thinking about suicide. You decide that it is the only way out of all the troubles. You will be out of your misery and your parents will see how wrong they have been and change their lives.

The problem is that if you committed suicide you would think that you would be doing everybody a favor. You wouldn't, because the minute you succeed there's nothing left of you. You're really thinking of yourself, and not anyone else.

In the end what would happen is that all your loved ones would be filled with guilt and resentment. They might try to hurt themselves in order to solve their problems, which won't do you or them any good either.

We know that right at that moment you don't want to face the world any longer because you may have seen so much that is bad. We know, too, that you probably feel responsible for your parents' problems because of things you have done, like:

Running away
Not listening to them
Not being home by the times they say

Or maybe you have heard your stepmother say to your father (or the other way around), "If your daughter [or son] wasn't here, I wouldn't be drinking like this." Then you think, "I knew it all the time."

If you're thinking this way, you are wrong. It is *not* your fault, and you can't make it better for your parents. Most likely if you are behaving badly it is because of *their* problems, not yours.

Believe us, getting mad and hurting yourself won't help your parents get rid of alcohol problems. If you think it will, we suggest you get out of the house for a while. Find a relative or friend, think and talk it out.

You have to look at it this way: You don't really want to die. Why end your life if you didn't do anything wrong (or even if you did)? Your life is so precious. There is only one of you, and you are special even if you *think* that no one else likes you. There are probably things you can do that no one else in the world can do. You just have to find your talents. You have to just keep working at it.

They Need Adult Help

What we are saying is that no matter what *you* do—whether you run away, dump out alcohol, or try to kill yourself—you can't convince your parents not to drink again. Keith said, "I never could. I tried to help my stepfather. I tried to talk to him about his problem, but it didn't help. He just had a mind of his own; it was like he said, 'Get out of my lane.' "

Your parents need professional help, or they need to talk to people who have been successful in stopping drinking and recovering. There are a number of organizations that can help. There are detoxification centers, residential treatment centers, mental health centers, as well as Alcoholics Anonymous—all easily available to anyone who needs help.

The best thing you can do for your parents is to support them in whatever decision they make for recovery, and to get some help for yourself.

Hitting Bottom

If running away, getting rid of alcohol, and hurting yourself doesn't cause alcoholic parents to give up alcohol, you might ask, "What *does* cause them to get help?"

Your alcoholic parents are like live souls trapped in dead bodies. Their minds are always trying to do what their bodies won't allow them to do. What we mean is that they are always trying to seek help, even though it might not seem that way to you.

Some parents *will* listen to their friends and relatives and go for help. A few *will* get help when they find themselves waking up every morning with hangovers or when their alcohol bills go way up.

But 90 percent of alcoholic parents will keep on drinking until things like *real* pressure from friends and relatives and, too often, tragedies push them into treatment, things like:

Death in the family
Car accident
Loss of driver's license
Marriage breakup
Loss of home because of nonpayment
Loss of job
Loss of children

Here are some examples.

Chet is a sixty-year-old man. He has been drinking ever since he was very young. He has tried to stop over and over, but has not been able. His family (his daughter and grandchildren) are getting increasingly impatient with his drinking and are encouraging him to find ways of getting help. He decides to try out Alcoholics Anonymous.

Pam is a single mother. One morning, after drinking heavily the night before, she wakes up in bed with a strange man. She looks at him and says, "Who are you and what are you doing here?" She realizes then that something has to be done. This was something that she would not normally do, and she must have been so drunk that she blacked out.

Margaret has been drinking for five years. Her drinking has reached the point where she is drinking in the morning. She has lost her job, and no one will hire her. She is married, with three kids, but her husband left her and took the kids and won't let her see them unless she stops drinking. She decides to go to an Alcoholics Anonymous meeting. Actually she was drunk, and a friend talked her into it. She keeps going to meetings because she really misses her kids and she wants to see them again.

Joe is a stepfather. One night he comes home drunk and goes into his stepsons' room. He wakes up the older one and begins to hit him. His stepson hits his head on the bedframe and goes into convulsions. His mother wakes up from all the racket. She rushes her son to the hospital, where he dies from internal bleeding. Joe is arrested and charged. He is so distraught from what he has done that he seeks help, finally, on his own.

These people have "hit bottom." Hitting bottom is a term that describes what happens to cause alcoholics to stop drinking. It is the point where they can no longer stand themselves and they decide to do something about their problems.

Dennis B., a recovering alcoholic we interviewed, described what hitting bottom meant to him. "I guess I was sick and tired of being sick and tired. I found myself being miserable with people who I shouldn't be miserable with—my family. You just can't go out drinking at night until twelve or one in the morning and wake up at seven in the morning and be all sparkly-eyed.

"Hitting bottom is hard to describe. All I can say is that once people get to the point where they just don't like what is happening to them anymore and they make the connection between what is going on in their lives and the consumption of alcohol, they will do anything to get rid of the pain."

Every alcoholic reaches a time when his or her drinking is too much and needs to be stopped. The important thing is that it has to be on the *alcoholic's* time. It is just like in school when you and your friends are doing poorly in some of your classes. Each of you will have a point where you begin to work harder. In our class, for Mike it is a D— in algebra, for Josey, an F in social studies, and for Kim a C in anything.

It is the same for your alcoholic parents. As Brenda Reynolds, one of the authors said, "For some the bottom will be losing jobs, for others losing their families and friends, and for a few, losing their lives. It seems that for every alcoholic, the problems have to get to one of these points."

What your alcoholic parents will do once they hit bottom depends. Some go for help at Alcoholics Anonymous meetings, some go to residential treatment centers, and a lot, at least at first, go "cold turkey."

Cold Turkey

Cold turkey, as far as your alcoholic parents are concerned, is not something to eat on bread with Miracle Whip. "Cold turkey" is a term used to describe a way of quitting drinking. It means that your alcoholic parents just stop drinking on their own, with no help from anyone else.

Let's say that your dad has been drinking a lot, maybe three six-packs of beer a day for the last five years. Then one day your sister gets killed by a drunk driver (not him) and dies. At that moment he realizes what he has been doing in his life and for some reason he starts to think your sister's death is his fault. He feels terrible.

So he quits drinking altogether and he goes cold turkey. He doesn't go to Alcoholics Anonymous, he doesn't go to a residential treatment center, he doesn't go to a counselor or a doctor. He just stops—period.

From your point of view, this is weird, because you are so used to him drunk all the time. Now, wham!—he is sober. Well, kind of sober.

When your parents first go cold turkey, they are not exactly themselves. You might come home from school and find them staring into midair and daydreaming. You may tell them something about your day and, after you are all done, they say something to the effect of, "What did you say?"

Sometimes, too, parents quitting drinking on their own can be scary if their bodies are so used to the alcohol that they go through withdrawal. Withdrawal is what happens to a person's body if it has become dependent on the alcohol for all of its energy and then the alcohol gets taken away. The alcohol has become the body's "food," and the body reacts in strange ways to not having it.

Some people hallucinate because of withdrawal. Hallucinations, according to the Random House Encyclopedia, are "Perceptual experiences without the appropriate sensory stimulations which can be viewed as falsifications of reality." In other words, hallucinations are tricks that people's brains play on them.

Maybe your parents will start seeing things. A twelve-year-old girl named Stephanie Fisher said, "I saw a guy on a television show who woke up once after going cold turkey and thought he was seeing bats attacking him. He thought that they were going to kill him."

Hallucinations are caused by a condition called "delirium tremens." Delirium tremens is "a serious condition occurring most often when alcohol is abruptly withdrawn from an alcoholic. It produces a loss of appetite, terrifying dreams, various mental and nervous-system disturbances, and if severe, delirium. In some 10 percent of cases, death occurs."

Dr. Loy told us more about delirium tremens. "It can occur forty-eight to seventy-seven hours after the alcoholic stops heavy drinking. It can last about three days. The younger you are, the more you have to drink to have it happen to you."

A relative of one of the authors described to us her experience when her brother went through delirium tremens. "The d.t.'s (as they are called) were something else. My brother would be lying strapped to the bed and calm as can be. Then all of a sudden he would think the whole bed was moving and he would go crazy.

"He was extremely strong. His wife and I could barely hold him down. We thought that he was going to rip out of the belt that held him down.

"Sometimes it was scary and I would cry. He would be acting like he was driving a car, working the brakes and screaming and yelling, or he would be yelling at their daughter, 'I told you not to do that!'

"Then the next minute he would be petting the dog or the cat. Then I would laugh. After being there forty-eight hours with no sleep, you have to laugh to keep from going crazy yourself.

"The amazing thing was that after all this—and it lasted for seventy-two hours—he didn't remember a thing."

Dr. Loy told us that people don't remember anything after it is over because their brains sort of shut down while it is happening.

Going cold turkey can be a good way to stop drinking for some people and not a good way for others. If your parent has enough willpower to stay away from all alcohol (and if he or she doesn't go through withdrawal), it could work.

Too often though, alcoholics who quit drinking by going cold turkey will go back to drinking. Your parents' getting help from other people may be better than doing it on their own, because where alcoholism is concerned, sometimes they just can't do it all by themselves.

Getting Some Help

There are better ways for your parents to start recovering from alcoholism than going it alone. For one thing, they can go to Alcoholics Anonymous meetings. According to Dennis B., a recovering alcoholic we interviewed, there are over one million people in the Alcoholics Anonymous Program right now.

The "anonymous" in Alcoholics Anonymous means not knowing. If we were anonymous you wouldn't know what we are or who we are. You wouldn't be able to identify us.

Being anonymous is the essence of Alcoholics Anonymous. Let's pretend that you were an alcoholic and you went to a meeting where you weren't anonymous, and somebody said over the radio that there was going to be an alcoholics meeting and they mentioned your name. You would be pretty embarrassed, because being alcoholic is a very personal thing.

Being anonymous is important to Alcoholics Anonymous so that you would feel secure in coming back to another meeting. If they weren't anonymous, you might feel too ashamed to come back for help.

Meetings occur many times during the week in many different places. They are usually announced in the newspaper in your town. There are two kinds of meetings, open and closed. Anyone can go to the open meetings, while the closed meetings are for recovering alcoholics. People in the program each have sponsors who are available day and night to help each other.

Getting involved in this program could be better for your parents because the meetings can help them to go through the recovery process slowly. Because of that, it will probably last longer.

Also, it will help them to meet people who have overcome problems with alcohol. Alcoholics Anonymous members know what it feels like to try to stop drinking and what it is like to really stop. They can help your parents take the stress off themselves when things happen and they become afraid that they will start drinking again.

Mark C. said, "When I finally went to my first meeting, I was worried that I wouldn't make it, that I would stop before I got in the door. When I went there I saw all the people who I used to drink with, who I thought had died. I thought, 'Oh wow, if they can do it I can do it.'

"I asked a question at the meeting, which became the topic of discussion for that day. The question was, 'How do you stay sober?' The answer was, 'One day at a time. You don't worry about yesterday because you can't change it and you don't worry about tomorrow because it may never get here.' "

Alcoholics Anonymous Is
Nothing Like We Imagined

When we first imagined going to an Alcoholics Anonymous meeting, we pictured a room full of bums, people who were dirt poor, or "bag people," people who weren't well dressed, or uneducated people.

A couple of us went to a meeting one day to see what it was like, and it wasn't like anything we had imagined.

At this meeting was a couple who were traveling around the country and who stopped in our town and came in for a visit. They were very well dressed. The man who was running the meeting that day was also well dressed. There were some people there who were poor, but mostly we saw a group of regular, everyday people making an effort to help themselves and each other.

Some people were younger, maybe in their early twenties, and some older, maybe in their sixties. The majority looked like they were in their thirties. There wasn't anybody there as young as us (except us).

We don't know if all of the people at this meeting were friends, but we know that some people who sat by each other seemed like friends. It seemed as if they were like a family in a way.

We were in a classroom. There were a couple of tables with chairs all around them and there were chairs surrounding the room as well. On one table there was coffee and cookies and cake.

We just sat in the room and listened while the meeting went on. It was an "open" meeting. There was a system to how the meeting was run. First there was a reading, and then someone picked a topic to talk about. The topic that was picked for this day was "gratitude."

Then the man who ran the meeting (it could be a woman; according to Dennis B., 30 percent of AA is made up of women) for that day picked people who wanted to talk about gratitude (no one *has* to talk). Once someone was picked—let's say it was a guy— he said his name like this: "My name is Bill, and I am an alcoholic."

Then everybody else in the room all at once said, "Hi, Bill." Bill then talked about something to do with gratitude. He talked about how glad he was to have everyone at the meeting and how it was nice they had each other.

Everyone else in the room listened to what Bill had to say, and then someone commented on it or said something similar to it, while others just listened quietly. After that another person spoke. We didn't hear anybody's last name while we were there.

One thing that stuck in our minds about the meeting we went

to was that one of the women there was celebrating her first anniversary; she had gone a whole year without drinking. Everyone at
the meeting encouraged her to stay sober, and some who hadn't
made it a year hoped that they could do the same thing. At the end
of the meeting they brought out a cake to help her celebrate.

There was a mixture of feelings in the air during the meeting.
The woman who was celebrating her anniversay was so happy that
she cried. Everybody seemed happy for her, yet they knew what she
had been through. She felt good that she had finally accomplished
something, and we felt happy for her.

The funny thing was that everybody celebrating her anniversary seemed like they were celebrating for themselves, too. It
seemed like they all got some support from it.

Another thing we noticed was that there were even some people there who had stopped drinking, then started up again, and
then stopped again, many times, and had never reached their first
anniversaries. This didn't seem to make any difference to the other
people there; it didn't seem to make them want to help these
people less.

No one said, "You are stupid and you shouldn't do this; you
are going to have to leave because you aren't working hard
enough." Instead, they just tried to be helpful. They were sympa-
thetic to what the problems were because they had all been in the
same boat at one time or another. It was as if they were thinking,
"Maybe this time they will stick to it."

For some of your parents, though, Alcoholics Anonymous
won't be enough to get them started on recovering. They may need
to go to a residential treatment center.

How Your Parents Might Get
to a Treatment Center

A residential treatment center is a place where your alcoholic
parents can go to get help to stop their drinking and to learn how to
live without alcohol. It is like a nursing home for alcoholics, and
your parents can go there when their drinking problems become so
severe (physically and emotionally) that they might die from them.

One of the important things about treatment centers is that alcoholics who go there don't come home at nights (usually for about a month). They don't even have the chance to drink while they are getting treatment.

Some people go to a center on their own, but many are sent by their employers, by the courts, or by their families (they still have to sign themselves in). Sometimes professional alcohol specialists can help families to get your parents into a center for treatment if they should completely refuse to go. Mr. O'Brien talked to us about something called an "intervention":

"If a family has an alcoholic who refuses help, there are some steps for these people to take. The first step is for the family to learn as much as they can about alcohol and alcohol abuse, like all of you are doing in this book. They do that by going to a lot of programs, by going to Al-Anon and Alateen, and by reading books. After this they can be organized to do what is called an intervention.

"What an intervention does is to bring as many people together as possible, to kind of gang up on the alcoholic, to get him or her to stop. To do this, the family has been prepared in certain ways. They have been taught how to confront the alcoholic in nonjudgmental ways. They will talk about specifics, like last night the person came home drunk, three weeks ago someone loaned their car and the alcoholic lost it because of drinking.

"They bring information and people together all at once to try to make it overwhelming to the alcoholic. They take care of all the details. If the person has a dog and is concerned about who is going to take care of the dog, they find someone to do that. They anticipate all the excuses. They set some consequences, some bottom lines if the person doesn't go to treatment. They make it so there is no choice, and that takes some work, but it is worth it if it is done right."

Once at the centers, your parents will go to therapy sessions and get involved in activities, all having to do with living without alcohol. There will be staff at the centers who will help them get over the aftereffects of stopping drinking, such as malnutrition and delirium tremens. There are staff who teach alcoholics what will happen to them if they keep drinking.

You Will Need to Go, Too

The other thing about your parents' going to a residential treatment center is that if your parents go you are going to have to go, too. This is because all family members need help. Everyone in the family is made sick by alcoholism in a different way, and the centers have people trained especially in family treatment who know how to talk to everyone.

You will be scared, and you will have weird images of the place. A lot of kids are afraid to go to treatment centers. When you think of a residential treatment center, what is the first thing you would think of?

A lot of people in white robes walking around?

A hospital?

When someone says an "alcoholic in a treatment center," what do you think of?

A violent man in his mid-thirties, eyes shot to hell, bad complexion, with a bottle in a paper bag?

If you said yes, don't feel bad, because we thought the same things, too. What we expected when we visited Conifer Park, a residential treatment center in Schenectady, New York, were jailhouse bars, strange people, and weird doctors, like you see on television.

We thought of people going into special rooms where they would receive shock treatments. They would have cups put all over their heads and then they would get zapped.

It wasn't like that at all. It was more like a mansion than a hospital. It was a really nice place, with a heated swimming pool and a sauna and a beautiful dining room.

There is another reason why you might not want to go to the treatment center with your parents. The night before your parents go you may lie in bed without being able to go to sleep, because if your parents have been drinking for a long time, maybe ever since you've been alive, you are probably excited about the possibility that things will finally change, but you may be upset, too.

In fact, you really may not know what to feel. You may be glad that your parents are going to get some help, because even if it doesn't do something good for you, it will be doing something good for your parents.

You could be upset because by the time your parents go to a treatment center for help you may have pretty much gotten to the point where you just don't care any longer.

It may just seem like you have been trying to help for so long and you have found out that you can't help and that they don't want your help (both of those things are true), and you have sort of given up. You don't want to get your hopes up (it has probably taken you a long time to get to the point where you think, "If it happens, it happens") because you know there is a good chance that nothing is going to change.

More than likely, you have heard for a long time from your parents how "things are going to get better." You have watched your parents stop and start drinking over and over and you know there is a possibility that your parents will walk into the treatment center and say, "I'm not going to do this," get scared, and walk right out. You may have been through that before.

You may even start to hope that your parents don't go through with the treatment center at all because of what could happen if they do fail. You may think, "It's true that my life seems bad, but I've grown accustomed to things the way they are. This is my family, and I don't know what any other family is like because I've never experienced one.

"I've already gotten used to just not really living at home. After school I go right over to a friend's house and I sleep over night every chance I get and, generally, spend so much time there that I might as well say they are my family.

"If Dad [or Mom] goes for help and fails, it's possible that they could come back grouchier. They could go out on a binge because they are upset about not being able to quit drinking."

You could be lying in bed, confused and afraid, and all these thoughts are rolling through your head. Probably on top of all of that you're wondering, "If it doesn't change this time, will it get worse?" or "What's going to happen the next time they try, or will there even be a next time?"

This is all normal. You shouldn't worry about it, because when and if your parent finally goes to a center you will probably be embarrassed and happy all at once. You won't want to tell your friends about it but you will be proud of your parents and glad that they are finally trying to get help.

You will see them sober and it will make you want to help them again. You will start feeling a little hope that something good is finally going to happen. Even if you are afraid or confused, you should go, because it's worth it whether your parents stay sober or not.

A School for Learning About Yourself

One way to think of a treatment center is as a school for learning about yourself. The most important thing that the staff at a treatment center does is to help people talk about their lives.

The center helps you and your parents mostly in groups. They have a lot of different groups for a lot of different problems. There are feelings groups, lecture groups, and education groups. They help people in groups so that the people can then help each other; people seem to learn best from what other people like them have to say.

At the center, the staff really tries to confront you and your parents with the fact that you have problems. Confronting means putting pressure on. They have found that if they do this, they can get people to face their problems.

We made up a play to show what we think it is like to be in an alcoholics group.

Group Therapy: A Play About Denial

Characters:

Group Leader
Mack

Jack

Nick

Don

Melodie

Group Leader: You are all alcoholics trying to recover, and that is why you are in this group. Some of you don't want to be here but are here. You have been told by someone that you have a problem, but you don't believe it.

Group Leader: We have a new member in the group today. Her name is Melodie. Would you stand up, please.

Melodie: Hi!

Group Leader: Would you like to tell the group how you got here?

Melodie: Well, I was picked up so many times for being drunk out on the streets that the court made me come. I didn't and still don't want to be here.

Group Leader: We understand that. It will take you a little bit of time to understand. You should listen to what everyone else has to say and maybe they can help you. Mack, today we will start out with you. You don't have to stand up, you can sit down.

Mack: Why me? My wife made me come.

Group Leader: Your wife made you come? Could you tell the group why she made you come?

Mack: She seems to think that I have this horrible problem. I really don't drink all that much. She just said that she was going to make me come or she was going to leave me. So I figured I would come and see what it's about.

Group Leader: What is this horrible problem she thinks you have?

Mack: She thinks I drink too much. I don't think I drink too much.

Group Leader: What do you think is drinking too much?

Mack: Drinking too much is being drunk a hundred percent of the time.

Group Leader: How much of the time are you drunk?

Mack: Only about seventy-five percent of the time.

Group Leader: Have you ever hurt anyone by being drunk?

Mack: Not severely.

Group Leader: Why do you think that your wife thinks it's important you're here?

Mack: I have *no* idea.

Group Leader: You haven't talked to her about it?

Mack: Maybe she just feels like being a pain in the butt, I don't know.

Group Leader: Does anyone have a definition of what an alcoholic is? You, Don, what do you think?

Don: Not being able to control your drinking.

Group Leader: Do you think it's true that Mack has to be drunk a hundred percent of the time to be alcoholic?

Don: No, he is definitely an alcoholic!

Mack: I am not!

Group Leader: All right, no fights here, guys.

Group Leader: So, Don, you really do think he is an alcoholic?

Don: Yes, he doesn't have any control over his drinking.

Mack: I have control!

Group Leader: Mack, what do you do for a living? You said seventy-five percent of the time you're drunk. What are you doing the rest of the time?

Mack: Sleep and eat.

Group Leader: Do you do anything productive?

Mack: Productive?

Group Leader: Like having a job?

Mack: My wife has a job.

Don: So you mooch off her.

Mack: No I don't.

Group Leader: Do you think that if you didn't drink seventy-five percent of the time, could you get a good job?

Mack: I could get a good job now.

Group Leader: Let's move on. Jack, why are you here?

Jack: My children sent me.

Group Leader: Your children? Did they tell you why they sent you?

Jack: Because they say that I always harass them.

Group Leader: Jack, Mack drinks seventy-five percent of the time. How much of the time do you drink?

Jack: Twenty-five percent.

Group Leader: Mack, do you think that he is an alcoholic?

Mack: No! I'm not an alcoholic and I drink seventy-five percent of the time, and he only drinks twenty-five percent of the time. He can't be an alcoholic.

Group Leader: Ummm. Okay. Nick, how long have you been drinking?

Nick: Two years.

Group Leader: Why did you start drinking?

Nick: Well, one night I came home and found out that my little daughter, about two years old, was walking down the road— she wasn't supposed to be, but she was—and she got hit by a car and she died. I felt so depressed I started drinking and drinking and I couldn't stop. I decided it was time to stop, so I came here.

Group Leader: So you came here on your own.

Mack: He must be crazy.

Treatment is a hard thing to go through. Mrs. S. described what she thought it was like for her brother to be at a residential treatment center. "It was hard. He didn't really want them to ask so many personal questions. They were trying to go way back in his life.

"He didn't like that they wanted to know and he didn't want to let them in. It was like, in his mind, it is none of their business what he did in his past. I could see him asking himself, 'What does it have to do with now?'

"I think that is what happened to him all day long. The staff was always trying to break those barriers. Toward the end he took what they called 'a walk.' This is where the staff turn the lights off and they let that one person talk, and he or she can say anything they want about his or her life. The person can talk right through from when he or she was little right up until the present.

"My brother hasn't told me about his walk yet; he said he wasn't ready. He has told me a lot of stories about the other people who were there, and I think it has helped him to realize that a lot of people are hurting. They need help just like him."

We asked one of the staff members at Conifer Park why recovering is so hard. He said, "No pain, no gain." What he meant was that if you are going through the treatment and you are not feeling anything, then you are not getting anywhere. He also said, "The actual drinking problem is harder than recovery, but in the beginning recovery is very hard."

When the Drinking First Stops

When your alcoholic parents do start to recover, it may seem at first that you and your family are about to have a better life. It may mean that you all could get closer and have more understanding among everyone.

As Kristin Rancourt said, it *is* much better to live with parents who do not get drunk anymore, because they can understand your feelings better; you can talk to them without them going out afterward and getting drunk; and you can trust them.

When your parents first quit drinking, you may not be sure that anything is going to get much better, because in the beginning you don't know exactly what your parents are going to do when they are sober.

You start to notice little things. Your parents take up annoying habits like smoking too much, drinking too much coffee, or eating lots of food. Of course, it *is* cheaper to buy food than alcohol. These habits are not as bad on the family as the drinking. These things make you afraid, though, that your parents could be different, and you are afraid that different will be meaner and stricter.

The truth is that in the beginning some parents become bitter. The bitterness comes from not having the alcohol in their lives anymore. Something has been taken away from them, something that was very important and a very big part of their lives. It seems to make them mad, and when they feel that way, they start blaming everyone around them, as if it is everyone else's fault.

Some of the bitterness comes also because your parents lose all the false confidence they had when they had "the bottle" in their lives. They got used to the alcohol making them feel comfortable around people and capable of doing their jobs. Now that they don't have that, it scares them.

Sometimes this bitterness is called being a "dry drunk." A dry drunk is a person who thinks the same and acts the same as when he or she was drinking.

It isn't much more fun having a dry drunk parent than it is having a drunken parent. You are so disappointed that nothing has seemingly happened or has changed.

It can be very depressing, because you think about how hard you have tried all the time your parents were drinking. You think about all the times you picked them up off the stairs after they fell down. You think about how they never even remembered what you had done for them and how, now, they are implying by their actions that they don't appreciate you. At least then you knew you were needed. Now you find yourself saying to yourself, "What do I do now?"

It feels so bad that you sometimes wish that your parents would start drinking again. When your parents get very irritable you may even do things to try to to get them drinking again. You feel bad about acting this way (you know it's better that your parents don't drink), but you just don't like being treated badly.

On top of that, your parents may still be having other problems.

While your alcoholic parents were drinking, your nonalcoholic parents felt like leaving them because they were so sick of the drinking and all the things that went with it.

Now, even after your parents have quit drinking, your nonalcoholic parents may still not know if they should leave because, with everything that has happened, they still don't trust your alcoholic parents not to start drinking again.

Even if they do trust them, their love may have changed. It is like the change in love you have for a new stuffed animal after the teddy bear you've had for a long time gets lost or thrown away. You just don't love it as much as you loved the other one, at least not right away. This will confuse you, because you thought that every problem would disappear when the alcohol was gone.

The important thing to remember is that your parents' problems are not *your* problems, and there are a lot of things you can do when they come up. You can cry, because crying makes you feel a lot better whenever you're frustrated. You can find somebody to talk to, like a good friend, because that always feels good.

Another thing to do when you feel like this is to find out more of what recovery is all about. You should get to know as much as you can. If you don't know what it's all about, you'll think that it's easier than it really is. You'll expect your alcoholic parents (and your nonalcoholic parents) to do more than they can do. You will think, Pooff! Everybody will be happy!

What Recovering Really Means

Recovery starts the moment your alcoholic parents stop drinking. Recovery is more than just not drinking, though. Recovery happens when your parents (and you) repair some of the damage that has been done and then get used to *living* without alcohol.

Recovery is physical *and* mental, because the alcohol problem is in the bottle and inside your parents. Frank Jones said, "My stepfather, in order to really recover, has to change his inner self as well as his outer self."

Your inner self is made up of many things. Susan Caffery, one of the authors, said, "It is your past in your memory, it is the ideas you really believe in, it is the truth that you think about the world of people around you, and it is what you think of yourself."

All these things combine to make up people's self-images. According to the Macmillan Dictionary, a self-image is "One's mental concept or picture of oneself, including an opinion of one's own abilities, the kind of person one is, and wants to be."

When your parents were drinking, they didn't have a good picture of themselves. Their worlds were small, in that they didn't really care about anything but themselves and their booze. That doesn't magically change when they stop drinking.

Recovery Is a New Way of Looking at the World

What we are saying is that your parents' recovery from alcoholism is really their learning another way of looking at the world, another way of seeing themselves.

Mark C. said, "The essence of recovery for me is realizing that I am powerless over alcohol. I cannot be around alcohol; I have to change everything in my life that ever dealt with alcohol, which means that I have to change everything, because everything I did involved alcohol.

"I met my wife, and we were drinking; we got married, we were drinking; we had the kids, we were drinking; we had the kids baptized, we were drinking; I met this friend, we were drinking; we did this or that, we were drinking. I have to realize that until I die I will be recovering. Only then will I be recovered."

Alcoholism has kept your parents from maturing. This means that in order to now grow up, they have to start from the beginning of the disease, just like somebody having amnesia for a number of years.

They have to learn a lot of things in order to recover. They have to learn responsibilities again (sometimes for the first time), things like doing their jobs, taking care of their kids, handling their money—all without alcohol. They have to learn things like courtesy, patience, and forgiveness.

As Jason Devens suggested, "Your parents spent a lot of time learning the alcoholic bad habits they have; it could take them a long time to unlearn these things." It is going to take a lot of patience for your alcoholic parents to recover: patience within themselves and within you, because the changes in them will come very slowly.

In the beginning especially you will have to be patient with your parents' moods. They will be moody. For example, you might tell them a joke that you think is funny, and they'll start crying.

One minute they'll be happy, the next minute sad, and then they'll be in between. Really, sometimes they won't know *what* they're feeling.

You see, when your parents were drinking, they could create their feelings with alcohol. Now that they are away from it, their real feelings are going to come out, and those feelings are going to go all over the place for a while.

You Can't Push Them

When your parents are first recovering, you will want to push them to go faster. The truth is that it is hard enough for your alcoholic parents to stop drinking. If they have people around them pushing, expecting them to do more, recover faster, it can be bad. All the pushing can actually push them to drink again.

You have to remind yourself that recovering from alcoholism is a process of going up and down. In the beginning, your parents will be very shaky, and it will be easy for them to start drinking again.

You have to remember that your alcoholic parents won't ever really "get better" from alcoholism. They can stop drinking, but the disease is something they will have to struggle with for the rest of their lives. Your parents will always have to say no to friends, to relatives, and to themselves when alcohol is offered, because they know what it will do to them.

Just because they have stopped drinking won't mean that they can't start again. Even if they haven't taken a drink in two or three years, they are alcoholics, and if they take one drink, they are bound to get going full steam again.

Mark C. said, "I don't think the urge to drink ever goes away completely. In the last six years since I have quit drinking, the urge has gotten less, and it is not so frequent. A lot of it depends on my mood. If I am under stress and strain, I might want a drink more than at other times."

You have to remember to try not to get your hopes too far up. You may start to think that they won't drink anymore, and sometimes they won't. Other times, when it seems to you that everything is going to be okay, your parents will go out and get drunk again.

This is called a "slip." A slip is when alcoholics who haven't been drinking go back to drinking. When it happens it is frustrating, and it makes you think, "Here we go again!" But it is a common part of the recovery process, and your parents may have many slips before they quit completely.

If you are pushing your parents, we know why. When your parents start to recover, it makes you really want to know more of what they're like when they're not drinking. You want to get to know them better. That is easy to understand.

When you feel like this, talk to yourself. Say, "They're trying, and someday they might recover. They might just get worse. In any case, I should be trying to get on with my own life instead of worrying about what they will do. I did that long enough, and it didn't do any good." When it happens, talk to your friends, get involved with a counselor, go to Al-Anon or Alateen meetings.

Don't forget, you have work to do, too.

You Have Recovering to Do, Too

Alcoholism is a family problem and because it is, you have to go through a recovery, an inner-self process, the same way that your parents do.

During those years of drinking, you and your family missed out on things in life like fun, loving, and caring, the helping each other out that goes along with being a family.

Because your life has been so torn for so long, you may have lost all your hope and faith. You may have even gotten to the point where you just don't feel anything anymore, not love, not hate. You may have begun to see yourself as no good and all adults as possible drunks.

There Are Still Feelings

This means that there are still feelings there, things you have to get over. You will have to work at these in order to forget the past and just live in the present.

In order to live in the present you will have to begin seeing your parents differently, as having their own personalities, not all bad or all good.

You will have to forgive them for things they did when they were drinking. This will not be easy to do, because they may not know what they did and what they did may have really, really hurt you. You will have to get over being afraid of your parents.

After your alcoholic parents quit drinking (and really, even if they don't), you'll have to get a totally different perception of yourself. You'll have to learn that you're not the bad kid your father or mother has described you as. You'll have to find ways to convince yourself that you are good and that you can be the things you want to be.

You'll Need Some Time and Patience

You may need some time to yourself, and you may need some help. Your parents may not realize it, but you need someone to talk to just like they do.

Counselors help you talk out your feelings. If you are someone who grew up in an alcoholic family, this is important, because you usually don't know what you are feeling.

Your parents have hidden their feelings with alcohol for years, and in the process they have taught you to hide yours without alcohol (at least in the beginning). Finding out your feelings will have a lot to do with your recovering.

Al-Anon and Alateen are programs like Alcoholics Anonymous, except they are for people who live with alcoholics (whether they are recovered or not). We interviewed a thirteen-year-old girl who recently began going to Alateen after her father went to a residential treatment center. She said that she would recommend Alateen for kids, both boys and girls. She told us, "When you first go to a meeting, someone will give you an introduction and will tell you how the program works. You don't have to go to every meeting. You can go when you need to.

"At each meeting someone reads a passage from a book, and then anyone can comment on whatever was read. Then somebody will talk about a problem. You don't have to talk if you don't want to. You can just sit there the whole time and listen.

"No one gives you advice. Other people just tell you things that they think would help you with your problem. If there is someone special at the meeting who you want to talk to, rather than telling the whole group what is on your mind, you can do that.

"It is useful. I learned about what it meant to be a dry drunk at one of the meetings, and I wouldn't have understood if I hadn't gone."

Just remember that getting your feelings out will require patience, too. You can only go so far so fast. You will never really forget what it was like living in an alcoholic family, but you can get past it and start to enjoy life.

You might feel sad and confused while you are going through this, but once that passes you may grow to like your parents (and yourself) more than you ever could have guessed, maybe more than if they had never had problems in the first place.

Epilogue

Now that you have read this book, we hope that you have learned more of what alcohol is and how it can effect your body and mind. We hope that it will be easier for you to decide to not take another drink—or your first.

We hope also that this book will help you if you are troubled and live in an alcoholic family. We want you to know that there is always hope, that no matter how bad it gets, you can still get better.

This is important, because if you believe that your life is terrible and you give up hope, life will just get worse. You need to know that you should not give up trying. You will be able to get help if you try hard enough.

We have tried our hardest in writing this book, and it has been good for many of us. It taught all of us in the group about alcoholism and alcohol—in detail. For one year we did nothing but eat, drink, and sleep the topic. When you do this it makes you really aware of what you are doing.

We now better understand the dangers of alcohol abuse and we think that we will be less likely to abuse alcohol. Because of this experience we will be more able to help friends if they abuse it.

For those of us in the group who have had to deal with alcoholism in our lives, it has been helpful learning about how others feel and how they handle the same kinds of problems that we do. It has been helpful to get our feelings out in the open to other people who know what we are talking about; it has helped us to feel less lonely.

We now know that people who are alcoholic are often good people. We know that their alcoholism is a disease and that they didn't become alcoholics because they were bad people but because they became addicted to alcohol.

It Wasn't Always Easy

It wasn't always easy to write this book. The first day was kind of scary, and there were plenty of times when it was boring, confusing, and just plain hard. All the questions that we had to answer made us have to be constantly thinking about things we didn't always know or understand. There were plenty of times we wanted to give up, times when we were burned out, when we had had so much of the subject that we couldn't stand to hear another thing about it.

Also, a lot of us in the group were really different from one another. This was both good and bad. It was good in that the project brought together people from different walks of life in a way that nobody had done before, and because of that we all got to meet new and different kinds of people who would talk about things that any one of us wouldn't have thought of on our own. When that happened, it made us think and learn.

Our differences were bad at times because we didn't always get along. Sometimes our differences were so strong that they caused problems and we didn't work as well together as we could have.

All in All, We Had Fun

However, all in all, we learned many different things and had a lot of fun. Despite the tensions and the bickering that sometimes completely stopped everything, everyone who started the project finished it.

The book itself kept us all together. We felt challenged from the beginning to finish it; we felt determined not to give up. In the Olympics you always hear people talking about "going for the gold," and that is kind of the way it was for us. We had a goal and we wanted to reach it. When we finally finished, it was like a load off our backs and we felt a real sense of accomplishment.

After it was all over, we found that we missed the meetings we used to have each week. They seemed to give us something to look forward to, and they gave a lot of us a sense of security about alcoholism, a sense that if someone in one of our families had an alcohol problem we would be able to handle it. We think what made us feel that way is that, in the group, we could say anything we wanted to. We didn't have to hold anything back.

We think that everybody who lives in an alcoholic family should go through something like this at least once in their lives. We know that if someone asked us, we would definitely do it again.

We all think that alcohol study should be part of everyone's education. Everyone needs places where they can learn, talk, and understand their feelings and problems related to alcohol. They need to do it in groups with others who share their points of view. Alcohol study is very important for teenagers because, as Julie Carey, a student in our school, said, "If you can't deal with alcohol, you can't deal with anything."

Book Reviews

Take My Walking Slow
Written by Gunella B. Norris
Published by Atheneum in 1970

This book is about Richie. Richie has a problem, and the problem is that his father is alcoholic. His father is always making promises that he doesn't keep, and he beats Richie. At the end of the book Richie gets so mad that he attacks his father and then leaves. His family is broken up by the alcoholism, and Richie has all sorts of problems with friends because of it, too. The best part of the book is where Richie makes friends with one of his enemies. This is a good book and could help kids decide not to drink.

Reviewed by Kim Peterson and Kristin Rancourt

The War on Villa Street
Written by Harry Mazer
Published by Delacorte Press in 1978

In this book a teenage boy tries to come to terms with his relationship with his abusive father. For example, the boy gets in fights with his father over his drunkenness. At one point in the story the boy is taking part in a Field Day and is doing well when his father shows up drunk, has a fight with him, and causes him to go from first place to third place. He is so embarrassed after the fight that he runs away and is afraid to return because he is afraid that his friends will make fun of him. When they don't, he's surprised and ends up making friends with a girl who didn't like him when school began. At the end of the book, the boy and his father make up and things start to get better.

This book is well written and makes for good reading for a teenager. I think it would help kids who live with alcoholic parents to deal with their feelings.

Reviewed by Danny Turcotte

The Boy Who Drank Too Much
Written by Shep Greene
Published by Dell Publishing in 1979

This is a story about a boy who is severely alcoholic and gets into an enormous amount of trouble because of it. Many of his problems come from the fact that his father is alcoholic and his parents break up. It is a really good book, and it should show kids whose parents are alcoholic what can happen to them if they don't get help.

Reviewed by Jason Devens

The Edge of Next Year
Written by Mary Stolz
Published by Harper & Row in 1974

In this book the mother of the main character, Orin, is killed in a car accident while his family is coming home from dinner one night. After this tragedy his father starts drinking and becomes a drunk. Meanwhile, Orin has to take care of his brother Victor and has problems with friends because of his family life. In the end of the book Orin's father decides to get help because he is afraid that he will lose his sons. The book ends with Orin dreaming of his life with a sober father.

The best part of this book was when Orin was finding all of his father's empty bottles. Some of the comments he made were very funny. This book could help kids who live in alcoholic families by giving them hope.

Reviewed by Mike Mahar

Heads You Win, Tails I Lose
Written by Isabelle Holland
Published by J. B. Lippincott Co. in 1973

The main person in this book is Melissa. Melissa is a teenager who is fat and who has parents who drink too much and fight. One day Melissa takes too many diet pills to try to get thin and flips out. She gets sick of listening to her parents fight at the dinner table and suggests that they get a divorce. Her father finally does leave, which makes her mother very unhappy and causes her to blame Melissa. Her mother keeps drinking, but her father goes into the hospital. This is actually the best part of the book, because Melissa is finally able to admit that she has a problem, too, when she goes into the hospital to see her father.

This is a good book and maybe could help teach kids how to cope with parents who drink too much, not by taking diet pills or even telling parents off as Melissa did, but by accepting the fact that they have problems, too.

Reviewed by Shane Squiers

Escape from Nowhere
Written by Jeannette Eyerly
Published by J. B. Lippincott Co. in 1969

Coming home and finding your mother drunk is nothing to joke about. Carla Devon's mother is an alcoholic and her father is away from home a lot and can't be home to deal with the problem. He refuses to admit that his wife has a problem at all, so Carla is faced with dealing with the problem on her own. She finds this very hard to do. As a result, she turns to drugs, not hard drugs like narcotics, just, she says, "Little stuff like pot." As the story goes on, being high seems natural to her, and she finds it makes her problems better for a while but that it doesn't make them disappear.

In the end Carla and her mother get much closer and end up with more understanding for each other. This book could help teach kids to deal with their problems and understand that drugs and alcohol only help for a while but just cause trouble in the end. It is excellent reading.

Reviewed by Heather Watson

Listen for the Fig Tree
Written by Sharon Bell Mathis
Published by The Viking Press, Inc., in 1974

The main character in this book is Marvina Johnson. Marvina must help her mother make it through Christmas, the time of year when her father was killed, without drinking so she won't kill or hurt herself. Her mother does begin to drink but is helped by Marvina's strength.

This book is so long and drawn out and kids may not be likely to finish it. If they did read the book, though, it would show them that no matter how hard things get, they have to keep trying and stay strong because it can be worth the effort.

Reviewed by Kim Whitman

My Dad Loves Me, My Dad Has a Disease
Written by Claudia Black
Published by MAC in 1979

This book is good. The reason it is good is that a little kid whose father or mother or even both are drunks would be able to read it. And by reading it they could see why drunken parents act the way they do. The pictures (the book is mostly pictures) are drawn by little kids, and that makes it good, too. It really gets across the point that alcoholism isn't pretty and that it can hurt you and the people you love. The best thing about the book is that it could help little kids to understand what is happening to them.

Reviewed by Susan Caffery and Melini Rogers

Under the Influence
Written by W. E. Butterworth
Published by Four Winds Press in 1979

This story is about a boy named Keith Stevens who is an alcoholic and gets into fights and car accidents. In one accident his girlfriend is killed. This book talks about what the alcohol does to his body and his life. He is able to admit to himself that he is alcoholic but he never is able to do anything about it. It was a good book because it was realistic and scary.

Reviewed by Melini Rogers

The Secret Everyone Knows
Written by Cathleen Brooks
Published by Joan B. Kroe–Operation Cork in 1977

The three people in this story (a mother, father, and daughter) all have drinking problems and they all go to get help. The best part of the book is when the daughter admits that she was taking chances with alcohol and that she was an alcoholic. It is a good book because it shows how hard it is to open up to people when you or someone in your family does have a drinking problem, but that you can do it.

Reviewed by Brenda Reynolds

Knock, Knock, Who's There?
Written by Elizabeth Winthrop
Published by Holiday House in 1978

The story starts out with a father dying of pneumonia and a mother starting to drink because of it. After his death no one in the family says very much about it. The boys in the story, Sam and Michael, take a long time to understand that their mother is drinking to hide her feelings. She gets into accidents and makes home life miserable because of it. Finally Kathleen, a good friend of Sam's, helps Sam to understand that his mother has a problem, although he doesn't want to believe it at first. Michael starts going to meetings at church and learns a lot of things about alcoholism that make him feel better, and he convinces Sam to go, too. The story ends with their mother starting to express her feelings through her paintings, and they believe that she will not drink again. This is a very good book.

Reviewed by Michelle Sandquist

The Late Great Me
Written by Sandra Scoppettone
Published by Longman Canada Limited in 1976

Geri Peter's mother always tells her that it's no good being "President of the leftover people," and that she should be popular and have a lot of friends. Geri is happy with her two friends until she meets Dave. Dave introduces Geri to alcohol, and Geri soon becomes hooked on it. She begins to do awful things when she's drunk, things that she doesn't remember the next day. After an incident where she hits a teacher when she's been drinking, people begin to realize that she has a problem. One person in particular, Kate, a teacher at Geri's school and a recovering alcoholic, convinces Geri to go to an Alcoholics Anonymous meeting. This becomes the beginning of Geri's recovery. Geri's mother begins to accept that Geri was fine the way she was and takes the pressure off her to be more popular. Geri goes back to her old friends and stays away from the ones who drink. Geri has not gotten rid of her alcoholic problem, she has just prevented it from continuing.

This book could be helpful to people who are doubtful of whether or not they are alcoholic, because they may be able to see familiar things in it to convince them of their problems. It also shows that popularity can get so important that you would hurt yourself to get it.

Reviewed by Kim Whitman